The Gospel of John

OneBook.

DAILY-WEEKLY

The Gospel of John

with **Ben Witherington III**

Scripture quotations, unless otherwise indicated, are taken from the Holy Bible, New International Version', NIV' Copyright © 1973, 1978, 1984, 2011 by Biblica, Inc.™ Used by permission. All rights reserved worldwide.

Scripture quotations marked NRSVACE are from the New Revised Standard Version Bible: Anglicised Catholic Edition, copyright © 1989, 1993, 1995 by the Division of Christian Education of the National Council of the Churches of Christ in the United States of America. Used by permission. All rights reserved.

Scripture quotations marked TLB or The Living Bible are taken from The Living Bible [computer file]/Kenneth N. Taylor.—electronic ed.—Wheaton: Tyndale House, 1997, c1971 by Tyndale House Publishers, Inc. Used by permission. All rights reserved.

Printed in the United States of America

Paperback ISBN: 978-1-62824-203-4
Mobi ISBN: 978-1-62824-204-1
ePub ISBN: 978-1-62824-205-8
uPDF ISBN: 978-1-62824-206-5

Library of Congress Control Number: 2015937052

Cover design by Nikabrik Design

SEEDBED PUBLISHING
Franklin, Tennessee
Seedbed.com
SOW FOR A GREAT AWAKENING

CONTENTS

Contents

Week Four
Jesus Heals a Man Born Blind   45

Week Five
The Good Shepherd and His Sheep   61

Week Six
Lazarus Raised from the Dead   74

Contents

WELCOME TO THE
ONEBOOK DAILY-WEEKLY

John Wesley, in a letter to one of his leaders, penned the following,

> O begin! Fix some part of every day for private exercises. You may acquire the taste which you have not: what is tedious at first, will afterwards be pleasant.
>
> Whether you like it or not, read and pray daily. It is for your life; there is no other way; else you will be a trifler all your days. . . . Do justice to your own soul; give it time and means to grow. Do not starve yourself any longer. Take up your cross and be a Christian altogether.

Rarely are our lives most shaped by our biggest ambitions and highest aspirations. Rather, our lives are most shaped, for better or for worse, by those small things we do every single day.

At Seedbed, our biggest ambition and highest aspiration is to resource the followers of Jesus to become lovers and doers of the Word of God every single day, to become people of One Book.

To that end, we have created the OneBook Daily-Weekly. First, it's important to understand what this is not: warm and fuzzy, sentimental devotions. If you engage the Daily-Weekly for any length of time, you will learn the Word of God. You will grow profoundly in your love for God, and you will become a passionate lover of people.

How does the Daily-Weekly work?

Daily. As the name implies, every day invites a short but substantive engagement with the Bible. Five days a week you will read a passage of Scripture followed by a short segment of teaching and closing with a question for reflection and self-examination. On the sixth day, you will review and reflect on the previous five days.

Weekly. Each week, on the seventh day, find a way to gather with at least one other person doing the study. Pursue the weekly guidance for gathering. Share learning, insight, encouragement, and most important, how the Holy Spirit is working in your lives.

That's it. When the twelve weeks are done, we will be ready with twelve more. Four times a year we will release a new edition of the Daily-Weekly. Over time, those who pursue this course of learning will develop a rich library of Bible learning resources for the long haul. Following is the plan for how we will work our way through the Bible.

The Gospels: Twelve weeks of the year the Daily-Weekly will delve into one of the Gospels, either in a broad overview or through a deep dive into a more focused segment of the text.

The Epistles: Twelve weeks of the year the Daily-Weekly will explore one of the letters, sermons, or the Acts of the Apostles that make up the rest of the New Testament.

The Wisdom Writings: Twelve weeks of the year the Daily-Weekly will lead us into some part of the Psalms, Proverbs, or prophetic writings.

The Old Testament: Twelve weeks of the year the Daily-Weekly will engage with some portion of the Books of Moses (Genesis–Deuteronomy), the historical books, or other writings from the Old Testament.

If you are looking for a substantive study to learn Scripture through a steadfast method, look no further. If it's sentimental and superficial you are after, there is no shortage of options elsewhere. The OneBook Daily-Weekly will also be available through the OneBook App. To learn more about how to access the app, please visit OneBookApp.com.

WEEK ONE

John 2:1–25

Jesus Changes Water into Wine and Clears the Temple Courts

INTRODUCTION

In John, the Fourth Gospel, we have a highly schematized presentation of the story of Jesus, with seven "I am" sayings linked to seven "I am" discourses, all presaged and prepared for by the seven sign narratives, which are miracle stories found in the first half of this gospel (between John chapters 2–12). Seven was the number of perfection, and lest we think the author just didn't have enough source material, he tells us clearly in the last verse of this gospel (John 21:25) that Jesus did many other things as well. So we have a carefully chosen and arranged series of materials, including miracle tales, in this gospel. Nothing happens by accident in Jesus' ministry—everything is ordered in a specific way to show the plan of God. Thus, in John 2, we have two crucial stories—the miracle at the wedding feast in Cana, and the action of Jesus in the temple. It is not clear whether the action in the temple was meant to be seen as a sign in the same way as the miracle at Cana, but as we shall see, both are symbolic actions.

Scholars have long noted that the placement of the temple story in John is at a very different juncture in the narrative compared to where the same story is placed in the other three canonical Gospels. In the latter, the story is part of the Passion narrative—the telling of the events that happened during the last week of Jesus' ministry. Here the story is found at the outset of the narrative. Why the difference? Concerning this event, most scholars would agree that: it did not likely happen twice; indeed, no single gospel suggests that it did (and if it had happened early in the ministry, it is hard to believe

1

Jesus would have even been allowed on the temple precincts thereafter by the Jewish officials); and the placement in the Fourth Gospel seems to be theological rather than chronological. One of the major themes of this gospel is that Jesus replaces or fulfills the major institutions in himself—he is the Passover Lamb, he is the Temple where God dwells, he is the purifying waters, he is the sacred bread, he is God's peace/Sabbath for humankind, and so on. The Fourth Evangelist wants to make this clear from the beginning of his story, and so he puts this temple action at the outset of his narrative.

One final point: the mother of Jesus appears in only two stories in this gospel—once at the outset of his ministry, and once at the conclusion, when he is on the cross. In a sense, then, the Evangelist presents Jesus in his relationship to his mother and his disciples together as bookend stories in this gospel. We will explore the reason for this later.

ONE

Wedding Faux Pas

John 2:1–5 *On the third day a wedding took place at Cana in Galilee. Jesus' mother was there, ²and Jesus and his disciples had also been invited to the wedding. ³When the wine was gone, Jesus' mother said to him, "They have no more wine." ⁴"Woman, why do you involve me?" Jesus replied. "My hour has not yet come." ⁵His mother said to the servants, "Do whatever he tells you."*

Understanding the Word. While scholars have debated which Cana might be referred to in John 2, it seems reasonably clear that it is the Cana that is about four miles from Nazareth, called Kefer Qana. It is possible that our Evangelist calls it "Cana in Galilee" to distinguish it from the Qana in Lebanon near Tyre. In any case, it was a small village, and the fact that Jesus' mother is there suggests it was near Nazareth and there may have been some family connections to the bride or bridegroom. A few background points will help in the understanding of this story.

Jewish weddings in Jesus' era went on for several days, and so it is not a surprise that the catering may have run out of one item or another. It would seem we join the story near the end of the wedding celebrations, long past the point in time when the best wine would have been served, which was at the beginning of the celebration, not near its end. The reason for this, of course, was that people had a more discriminating palette before, rather than after, the wine dulled their sense. Wine in Jesus' day was definitely alcoholic, involving fermented grape juice, though we cannot be sure of what sort of percentage of alcohol it would have had (ranging from a possible low of 2 percent to a high of 12–13 percent). To be sure, no toastmaster at a Jewish wedding would ever have said, "Why did you save the best grape juice until last?" The issue was real wine, and more to the point, wine that was not watered down. The normal practice was to water down the wine the further the celebrations went, to prevent complete inebriation. And so, of course, the best-tasting wine, rather than the watered-down sort, would be served first.

We are told that Jesus' mother is a wedding guest, but Jesus and some of his disciples were wedding guests as well. Jesus' mother in this gospel is never named, never called Mary. For the Evangelist her whole importance is in her relationship to Jesus. Here, and in John 19, she is simply identified as the mother of Jesus. It is true that the only reason anybody shows up in these stories in the gospel is because they have come across Jesus' path at some point, but Jesus' mother is a special case.

Acting like a good worrying mother, not wanting something to spoil the wedding party, she informs Jesus that they have no more wine. This statement, which implies a request—namely, "Do something about it!"—also implies that Mary knew Jesus *could* do something, something miraculous. Even though this is the first miracle story in this gospel, it implies that there had been other miracles beforehand, miracles known to Mary. The fact that the miracle at the wedding feast is the first sign miracle in this gospel has more to do with the Evangelist's theological schema. He will present a crescendo of the miraculous beginning with turning water into wine and finishing in John 11 with the raising of a man from death who has been in the grave four days. Jesus' response to his mother is somewhat shocking—it is abrupt, and almost seems like a rebuke. It literally reads "Woman, what to me and to you? My hour has not yet come." This brief Greek phrase likely means something like "What's that got to do with us?" (We are only invited guests, not hosts.) Notice that Jesus distances himself from his mother's authority, which is probably why he calls her "woman," which is surprising. In this gospel, Jesus must follow the dictates of his heavenly Father, not his earthly mother. But Jesus then gives a reason for his response—"my hour has not yet come." The hour referred to is not just any hour, but what we might call prime time. Later in this gospel, it refers to the time for Jesus to fully reveal himself to the world by dying on the cross.

Undaunted, Mary, who apparently will not take no for an answer, even from Jesus, tells the servants—"Do whatever he tells you." Apparently she does not take his rather brusque response as a definite no.

1. What sort of relationship between Jesus and his mother does this story depict?

2. Why has the wedding party run out of wine?

3. What does Jesus mean by "my hour"?

TWO
Saving the Best for Last

John 2:6–10 *Nearby stood six stone water jars, the kind used by the Jews for ceremonial washing, each holding from twenty to thirty gallons. ⁷Jesus said to the servants, "Fill the jars with water"; so they filled them to the brim. ⁸Then he told them, "Now draw some out and take it to the master of the banquet." They did so, ⁹and the master of the banquet tasted the water that had been turned into wine. He did not realize where it had come from, though the servants who had drawn the water knew. Then he called the bridegroom aside ¹⁰and said, "Everyone brings out the choice wine first and then the cheaper wine after the guests have had too much to drink; but you have saved the best till now."*

Understanding the Word. Recent archaeological work in and around Cana has unearthed numerous *mikvaoth*—ritual purification pools where Jews would go to remove ceremonial uncleanness. The six stone water jars in our story were for holding just such purification water for ceremonial cleansing. The picture of Jews in this region is that they were often devout, and particular about keeping the laws regarding clean and unclean. This family for whom the wedding is held was certainly a Torah-observant family. We are told that each stone jar (stone because according to Jewish thinking it could not become unclean or polluted) could hold twenty to thirty gallons! And Jesus was about to turn it all to wine! It may well be this story that got Jesus the reputation that he was "a drunkard" as well as a "friend of tax collectors and sinners" (Matt. 11:19). Whatever else you say about Jesus, he seems to have spent more time during the ministry feasting than fasting, and in this regard he stood apart from the praxis of his cousin John the Baptizer. The image of Jesus here is not of a killjoy, more nearly the life of the party, or at least the one who gives life to the party.

Notice that the only ones in the story who know a miracle has happened are Jesus, his mother, the disciples, and the servants involved in filling the jars with water and then dipping the new wine out to take to the toast-master. Despite the fact that the miracles in this gospel are stupendous, the Evangelist does not suggest that Jesus used miracles to wow people into the kingdom of God. He does reveal some of his glory to a select few in this story, but he does not make a big deal of the miracle or even make a pronouncement explaining it and taking credit. The impression all four Gospels give is that Jesus' main ministry was preaching and teaching, and he set out to various places for that purpose. But where a need arose, as was at this wedding, he was prepared to stay to heal or help. This is presumably because Jesus knew that miracles were, at best, temporary solutions or cures, whereas the acceptance of the gospel message was the key to having everlasting life.

Nothing happens in these Johannine stories by accident, and the climax where we hear "but you have saved the best till now" is a double entendre—it refers not only to the best wine served last at this wedding party, but it likely also reminds that God, after a long line of prophets, priests, and kings, has finally sent his Son to rescue the world. What he brings is the new wine of the gospel, the new wine of salvation, which is truly the best wine of all. And note that there is more than enough of it for all as well. More to the point, Jesus replaces the old, lifeless ceremonial water, which could do no more than cleanse the outside of a person, with the new wine of the gospel, which can make the heart glad.

1. Why doesn't Jesus make more of a public display and explanation of this miracle?

2. What does Jesus' turning of water into actual wine tell you about him? Was he an ascetic like his cousin John?

3. Why is the toastmaster so surprised at the outcome of Jesus' action?

THREE
Trailing Clouds of Glory

John 2:11–12 *What Jesus did here in Cana of Galilee was the first of the signs through which he revealed his glory; and his disciples believed in him. [12]After this he went down to Capernaum with his mother and brothers and his disciples. There they stayed for a few days.*

Understanding the Word. The culmination of the story tells us that this was the first of Jesus' semi-public sign miracles, revealing his glory, and that it was the disciples themselves who believed in him. We must be careful not to download all of the later Christian faith into the word *believe* when we hear something like verse 11. Here it likely means they came to believe what Mary already knew—namely, that Jesus could perform miracles. Throughout this gospel there is not only a crescendo of the miraculous, but there is also a crescendo of confessions of who Jesus is. The resurrection of Jesus is the climactic miracle (foreshadowed by the last sign narrative about the raising of Lazarus) and is followed finally by a confession of "my Lord and my God" by Thomas, which matches up with what the prologue in John 1 says about Jesus. Ironically it is only unbelieving Thomas's confession after seeing that proves to be a fully adequate confession of who Jesus is.

Verse 12 is interesting because it suggests that we are in a period of overlap between the time that Jesus was still at home with his family as an adult, and when he left his family behind and traveled with his disciples. This then would be a story from very early in Jesus' ministerial career. Notice it is Capernaum (or more properly, Kefer Nahum—the village of the prophet Nahum) where they go. Capernaum was to become Jesus' base of operations, probably based in the home of Peter's mother-in-law (which can possibly be seen today underneath the modern Franciscan church at Capernaum). This story should be compared to Mark 3:21, 31–35, where Jesus distances himself from his physical family because they not only fail to understand him; they are even worried (based probably on the exorcisms) that Jesus is playing with fire, or as the text suggests, is not in his right mind. The story of Jesus and his relationship with his brothers is even more problematic than that with his mother. As John 7:5 will inform us, Jesus' brothers did not believe in him during his ministry. This did not mean they didn't believe he could do remarkable miracles, like the one at Cana. It meant that they didn't think that he was the Messiah, the Savior of the world. It was only after Easter, and because of an appearance of the risen Jesus specifically to his brother James, that this situation seems to have changed (see 1 Cor. 15:7). Acts 1:14 tells us there is a happy ending to this story, for we find Mary and the brothers in the Upper Room, praying in preparation for Pentecost with the other disciples. This is the last direct reference to Mary in the Gospels and in Acts, and perhaps the last one in the whole New Testament.

1. What do you make of Jesus' relationship with his brothers? Compare it to the relationship of Joseph with his brothers in Genesis.

2. What does "believe" seem to mean in John 2?

3. The term "glory" comes up a good deal in the Fourth Gospel (see, for example, John 1:14—"we have seen his glory"). What do you think it refers to?

FOUR

Temple Tantrum

John 2:13–17 *When it was almost time for the Jewish Passover, Jesus went up to Jerusalem. ¹⁴In the temple courts he found people selling cattle, sheep and doves, and others sitting at tables exchanging money. ¹⁵So he made a whip out of cords, and drove all from the temple courts, both sheep and cattle; he* *scattered the coins of the money changers and overturned their tables. ¹⁶To those who sold doves he said, "Get these out of here! Stop turning my Father's house into a market!" ¹⁷His disciples remembered that it is written: "Zeal for your house will consume me."*

Understanding the Word. The story of Jesus' cleansing of the temple requires some background information to be fully understood. The court where they were selling sacrificial animals and changing money was the outer court of the temple, otherwise known as the Court of the Gentiles. This was the only place in the temple non-Jews were allowed to come and pray or offer sacrifices, and it was a relatively new thing for the Jewish temple officials to make available animals for sale in the temple precincts. Previously, such animals had only been sold in places like the Mount of Olives, but apparently the Jewish officials figured out a way to make a little more money for the temple treasury (especially important since the building of the temple proper was still continuing all the way up to the Jewish war in the AD 60s). Jesus sees this as a defiling of the temple, turning it into a marketplace. This reminds me of the church I once visited who had a senior minister who thought it was a good idea to install an ATM machine in the vestibule of the sanctuary "in case people forgot to bring money to give to the church." I was present at the meeting the Monday after this item was installed and, needless to say, the huge negative reaction to a mechanical but literal money changer in the temple led to its immediate removal.

The money changers were needed because the proper coin for paying the temple tax was the Tyrian shekel, which had the purest silver in it. This coin had a picture of Herakles (Hercules) on one side, and the royal eagle on the other, neither of which images would have failed to offend devout Jews. Nevertheless, these were the coins that the Jewish authorities required for the tax.

Jesus' reaction to these activities is dramatic, but we need to bear in mind it was not actually a cleansing of all the temple, which would have involved other courts as well and presumably the temple treasury itself, with its pagan coins. This is what is called a prophetic sign act, rather than a true full cleansing. It symbolized not only the need for reform, but it probably symbolized the coming judgment of God on Herod's temple, which Jesus clearly predicts in Mark 13, where he says it will happen within a generation (i.e., forty years). In fact, the temple became the temple of doom exactly forty years after Jesus' death in AD 30.

We are told that later the disciples remembered Psalm 69:9—"Zeal for your house consumes me"—which is spoken by God in the psalm. Here, it is used of Jesus himself to explain his actions. The implication is that Jesus is acting for God, or better said, as God himself. The theme of memory is important in this gospel. We are told in John 14–17 that the Spirit gradually leads disciples into all truth, and so here we see an instance of where the event happened at one point, but the spiritual understanding of its significance did not come until after Pentecost. This is true of many of the things that Jesus said and did, and perhaps we should not be too hard on the disciples. After all, they did not yet have the Holy Spirit during Jesus' ministry; they were only Christians under construction, learners in the school of Jesus.

1. Do you think this action of Jesus was inconsistent with his teachings about nonviolence in the Sermon on the Mount? If not, why not? Is there a difference between using force and acting violently toward another human being?

2. Why were the animal salesmen and the money changers situated in the temple precincts? What court did they occupy?

3. When is zeal for God's house a good thing and when can it go too far?

FIVE

A Temple Raised in Record Time

John 2:18–25 *The Jews then responded to him, "What sign can you show us to prove your authority to do all this?" ¹⁹Jesus answered them, "Destroy this temple, and I will raise it again in three days." ²⁰They replied, "It has taken forty-six years to build this temple, and you are going to raise it in three days?" ²¹But the temple he had spoken of was his body. ²²After he was raised from the dead, his disciples recalled what he had said. Then they believed the scripture and the words that Jesus had spoken. ²³Now while he* *was in Jerusalem at the Passover Festival, many people saw the signs he was performing and believed in his name. ²⁴But Jesus would not entrust himself to them, for he knew all people. ²⁵He did not need any testimony about mankind, for he knew what was in each person.*

Understanding the Word. The word *sign* in some contexts can refer to a proof or a validating sign, and that is what it means in this segment of the story. The Jews, which here means the Jewish officials, ask for proof that Jesus has the authority to cleanse the temple.

Cryptically, Jesus responds, "Destroy this temple, and I will raise it again in three days." This saying shows up in the trial of Jesus in a garbled form (see Mark 14:58) as an accusation against Jesus, so we can be pretty sure he did say something like this. Of course, the authorities were likely to take Jesus literally and therefore think that he had lost his mind. Thus far, it had taken forty-six years to build Herod's temple (which suggests the building began somewhere around 16 BC before Herod died), and it was nowhere near finished. Any threat to the temple was a threat to the local economy because the number one employer of laborers in Jerusalem was the temple, with its ambitious building projects.

The Evangelist, in verse 21, provides commentary saying that Jesus was not referring to Herod's temple, but to his own body as the place where God dwelt on earth while he was there.

In verse 22, we have another indication of after-the-fact clarity; the disciples brought to mind what Jesus said and understood it only after he rose from the dead. On the occasion itself, the actions probably prompted head-scratching and it may have fired up the more zealotic of the disciples, who wanted Jesus to be a military messiah like David. If this is what they thought after the triumphal entry on a donkey and then the temple cleansing, they would be disabused of this misunderstanding by the end of the week, and it would lead to disillusionment—all of the Twelve either denied, betrayed, or deserted Jesus before Thursday night was over. And then, of course, we have the revealing story of the trip down Emmaus Road by two former disciples leaving town (Luke 24), who ironically tell the risen Jesus "We *had hoped* [past tense] he would be the one who was going to redeem Israel," but the crucifixion had crushed such hopes.

Notice as well that we are told that the disciples came to believe both Scripture and the words of Jesus. The early church would later put these two things together as their sacred writings.

The story ends on an intriguing note with our being told that many believed in Jesus because of the signs he performed in and around Jerusalem (presumably some of the miracles as well as the temple cleansing), but clearly what they believed was that Jesus was a miracle-worker. The phrase "believed in his name" probably means no more than believed in the miraculous power of his name and person. They did not believe he was the Son of God and the Savior, which explains why the story concludes by saying that Jesus knew what was and was not in such people's hearts, and so he did not entrust himself to them.

1. What temple was Jesus most concerned with, and why did he correctly predict the downfall of both Herod's temple and his own?

2. What was the key to the disciples' later understanding of Scripture and Jesus' own words?

3. Why did Jesus not entrust himself to these new believers in his name?

COMMENTARY NOTES

General Comments. All seven of the miracle stories in John are worth studying. One consistent feature in all of them is that we do not see any particular interest in describing *how* the miracles happen, or for that matter, any interest in the miracles themselves. The interest is in what they point to outside of themselves—namely, the presence of King Jesus.

There are a variety of kinds of miracles in the Gospels; the miracle in John 2 is a nature miracle, so called because it involves doing something miraculous with inanimate matter. Other nature miracles would be the cursing of the fig tree (the only negative miracle in the Gospels), the walking on water, and presumably the multiplication of the loaves and fishes. Other types of miracles include: healings of various sorts; exorcisms; and raising people from the dead. It is notable that in this gospel there are no exorcisms at all. Furthermore, there is only one ministry miracle tandem in this gospel that is also found in the Synoptic Gospels—namely, the feeding of the five thousand coupled with Jesus' walking on water. Synoptic Gospels, or Synoptics, refers to the gospels of Matthew, Mark, and Luke. They are so called because they contain much of the same material and often in the same order. This gospel writer does not focus on Galilean miracles in the same way or to the same degree that the Synoptics do. Instead, he tells us unique stories about

miracles in and around Jerusalem and its suburbs, such as Bethany. Instead we have the healing of the cripple at the pool of Bethesda (John 5), the healing of the man born blind (John 9), and the raising of Lazarus (John 11). To judge from the miracle stories, this gospel was likely written by a Judean disciple of Jesus, and one with a connection to Mary. I would suggest that the person in question is the Beloved Disciple, who is probably not John son of Zebedee, not least because none of the special Zebedee stories are found in this gospel—not the calling of the Zebedees by the lake, not their witnessing of the raising of Jairus's daughter, not their presence at the transfiguration, and not their request for the box seats in the kingdom. Indeed the name Zebedee itself never comes up in the Fourth Gospel, save once, in the appendix in passing in John 21.

Miracles in the Fourth Gospel bear witness to who Jesus truly is, but do not provide absolute proof that he is divine, not least because prophets before Jesus and the apostles after Jesus performed many of the very same sort of miracles, including raising the dead. One cannot be impressed into the kingdom of God; rather, one has to embrace the truth by faith (as the purpose statement in John 20 suggests). In fact, in this gospel Jesus says that the disciples will one day do greater works than he has done, and this probably includes the signs or miracles. The story of Thomas in John 20 is a cautionary tale. He represents the seeing-leads-to-believing crowd. And Jesus will turn around and say that it is *believing* that truly leads to seeing.

Day 3. In the Fourth Gospel these miracles are called *semeion* (signs), whereas in the Synoptics they are called *dunameis* (mighty works). A sign, by its very nature, points outside of itself to something more important—in this case to the fact that Jesus, the Son of God, is on the scene.

The term *doxa* (glory), from which we get doxology, has as its Hebrew equivalent *Shekinah*, which refers to the shining presence of God, or better said, the bright physical manifestation of the presence of God when he comes into close encounter with human beings. Glory does not normally refer in the New Testament to fame or fortune or human accomplishments; it refers to an attribute or effect of God and his presence. It seems probable that when the gospel writer said, "We have seen his glory" or "Jesus revealed his glory," what he meant is that they had seen evidence that Jesus was indeed God incarnate, a manifestation of the divine in human form.

Day 5, verse 21. Notably, there are more parenthetical explanations by the Evangelist in this gospel than in any other gospel, again probably because it was intended to be used in evangelism and to train converts, or new disciples.

WEEK ONE

GATHERING DISCUSSION OUTLINE

A. Open session in prayer.

B. View video for this week's readings.

C. What general impressions and thoughts do you have after considering the video, readings, and the daily writings on these Scriptures?

D. Discuss questions based on the daily readings.

    1. **KEY OBSERVATION:** The two very different stories in this chapter reveal a Jesus who performs signs (both miraculous and prophetic), and yet he does not entrust himself to those who believe in his name based on such actions.

    DISCUSSION QUESTION: What should this teach us about making assumptions about who counts as a genuine follower of Jesus and who doesn't?

    2. **KEY OBSERVATION:** It is hard to miss Jesus' impatience with the Jewish authorities, who think that they know better than Jesus and understand him when they don't. Corruption in the house of God (or in the ministry) is the last place one should find such a thing.

    DISCUSSION QUESTION: If the religious leaders become corrupt, what happens to their followers?

    3. **KEY OBSERVATION:** In these two stories in John 2, we see the gamut of emotions of Jesus, from joy and celebration to anger and forceful action.

DISCUSSION QUESTION: What questions do both of these stories raise about Jesus?

4. **KEY OBSERVATION:** The signs and miracles of Jesus were only the undercard to the main event—the death and miraculous raising of Jesus.

   DISCUSSION QUESTION: Why do you think all four Evangelists spend a third or more of their total narrative on the last week of Jesus' life?

5. **KEY OBSERVATION:** The last story of John 2 tells us that there is an appropriate time and place for confrontation of evil in the house of God, of corruption in the clergy.

   DISCUSSION QUESTION: Can you think of a modern-day example of confrontation of corruption in the clergy?

E. What facts and information presented in the commentary portion of the lesson help you understand the weekly Scripture?

F. Close session with prayer.

WEEK TWO

John 3:1-21

Jesus Teaches Nicodemus

INTRODUCTION

As in other narratives in the Gospel of John, the Evangelist focused on an exchange with a specific kind of dialogue partner Jesus sometimes had, in this case a fellow Jewish teacher. The discussion is in many ways surprising because Jesus is not talking to Nicodemus about converts to Judaism from the Gentile world, or even proselytes who had begun the process of becoming Jewish, nor is he talking with a lapsed or nonpracticing Jew. To the contrary, he is talking with a devout Jew, indeed, a Jewish teacher like himself. To understand this dialogue and the pronouncements by the Evangelist which follow them, one has to realize that most ancient peoples, including most Jews, did not believe in what Christians would call conversion. By that, I mean a radical transformation of one's nature and worldview that leads to a change in one's beliefs and behaviors and religious practices. The question about a second birth by a clearly shocked Nicodemus reflects, in part, this reality. Ancient peoples believed that geography, gender, and generation (who one was a descendant of) largely determined a person's identity from birth. You were born with a certain identity and stuck with it. A person didn't become a Jew; one was born a Jew, unless one was prepared to go through an arduous socialization program ending in circumcision and keeping the entire Mosaic law. Jesus, however, clearly did believe people could change, could be "born again," and so did early Christians like Paul (see 2 Cor. 5:17). One of the major teaching aims of this lesson must involve a frank discussion about conversion, its nature and varieties, how it happens, and what are its implications.

16

A second major focus of this text is on the character of God, and God's desire to save the world, not to condemn the world. But salvation involves and requires sacrifice, the sacrifice of God's only begotten Son. Thus, another of the major teaching aims of this week's session must focus on both the character of God, and the important question in regard to the death of Jesus—why was death on a cross necessary for the salvation of the world? Couldn't God just forgive everyone without the drastic sacrifice of his Son? What kind of loving God puts his only natural child through a death like that—unless of course it was absolutely necessary for human salvation?

ONE

Night Vision

John 3:1–3 *Now there was a Pharisee, a man named Nicodemus who was a member of the Jewish ruling council.* *²He came to Jesus at night and said, "Rabbi, we know that you are a teacher who has come from God. For no one could perform the signs you are doing if God were not with him." ³Jesus replied, "Very truly I tell you, no one can see the kingdom of God unless they are born again."*

Understanding the Word. Pharisees were in many ways the very sort of Jews that were most like Jesus in their belief system. For one thing, they both believed in bodily resurrection as God's final remedy for disease, decay, and death. For another, Pharisees were part of a holiness movement. Like Jesus and his disciples, both were utterly convinced that Israel needed to change and be more faithful to the God of the Bible, more holy or sanctified in their behavior and praxis. But there the similarities mostly come to an end. The Pharisees thought that the way to revive and restore Israel was by taking a priesthood-of-all-believers approach—by which I mean, applying all the laws in Leviticus, formerly mostly applied just to priests, and requiring all Jews to live like priests when it came not only to food laws and Sabbath-keeping, but a whole host of other purity regulations and related strictures. Jesus, by contrast, called Jews not to believe and obey the Gospel of Leviticus, but rather, to become his disciples and take up the yoke of Jesus' teaching, some of which was radically new, and some of which reaffirmed and even intensified the most fundamental teachings of the Mosaic law (such as wholehearted love for God and neighbor).

I like to call this episode Nic at Nite, as that is when this dialogue takes place. And notice that Nicodemus is not just any Jewish teacher, but a teacher in Jerusalem who is a member of the Sanhedrin, the ruling council of the nation. Clearly, Nicodemus has heard impressive things about Jesus' sign miracles. (Though how he has heard about such things, and which signs, we do not know. Thus far in John, there have only been a couple of miracle narratives involving Jesus.) Nicodemus sees Jesus as a man who has come from God, one who has divine power and authority. Of course, he does not literally see how that was true (see John 1). Early Jews were not expecting a divine Messiah, a man who came *as* God. Perhaps Nicodemus had seen a sign miracle, but Jesus' response turned the conversation in a whole new direction. Jesus spoke about *seeing* the kingdom of God.

What is the kingdom of God? When we think of kingdoms we think of realms, places, and nations. The Greek term *basileia* used here (*malkuta* in the Aramaic original) can refer to a reign or a realm. Here Jesus would seem to be talking about the future kingdom coming on earth as it is in heaven, and so a realm. He talks about entering it as well. The implication is, even Nicodemus will have to change to see, much less to enter, the future coming kingdom of God. But what sort of change is involved?

Jesus said that even this respected Jewish teacher had to be "born again," or another possible translation would be "born from above." In fact, the rebirth Jesus is talking about is both a second birth and a birth from above. As we shall see, Nicodemus took Jesus literally, and so he is astounded at this demand.

1. Why did ancient peoples have doubts about the whole notion of conversion?

2. What impressed Nicodemus about Jesus' fledgling ministry?

3. What do you think Jesus meant by "see the kingdom of God" and being born again?

TWO

Twice Born

John 3:4–8 *"How can someone be born when they are old?" Nicodemus asked. "Surely they cannot enter a second time into their mother's womb to be born!" ⁵Jesus answered, "Very truly I tell you, no one can enter the kingdom of God unless they are born of water and the Spirit. ⁶Flesh gives birth to flesh, but the Spirit gives birth to spirit. ⁷You should not be surprised at my saying, 'You must be born again.' ⁸The wind blows wherever it pleases. You hear its sound, but you cannot tell where it comes from or where it is going. So it is with everyone born of the Spirit."*

Understanding the Word. One of the major repeated motifs of the Gospel of John is that there are often two levels of discourse. By this I mean that Jesus is often talking at one level, a more metaphorical or transcendent level, whereas his listeners take him to be speaking literally. This, of course, is a normal problem for those who believe in the Bible, like Nicodemus, and tend to take it literally, perhaps too much of the time. Nicodemus is clearly stunned by the demand that he be born again especially when, as he says, he is an old man. Perhaps he was thinking, *You can't teach old dogs, new tricks,* as we might put it. What he actually says is "Surely you can't crawl back into your mother's womb and call for womb service!" He's thinking entirely of a second physical birth, not a spiritual rebirth.

Jesus, in response, tells him how this can happen and why it must happen. In order to enter the final reign of God upon the earth, for which Jews like Nicodemus fervently prayed, in order to enter the restored earth, the restored divine realm at the end of human history after the resurrection, one first must be born again, and this time Jesus says quite literally, "born of water and the Spirit."

Scholars have debated for centuries what Jesus is referring to here, and later Christian commentators even suggested he was talking about what happens at Christian baptism! This, however, is clearly an impossible interpretation of this text if it reflects an actual conversation between Jesus and Nicodemus. When they spoke to one another, there was no such thing as either Christianity or Christian baptism. No, this is a discussion about birth by some other means, and here we need a little help from the larger Jewish context to understand this conversation. A birth of water in early Judaism would quite readily be understood to refer to physical birth, with the breaking of the mother's water and then the emergence of the child. But what of the birth of or by means of the Spirit? It is the latter Jesus is really focusing on here.

Jesus draws an analogy between the Holy Spirit and his work and the wind. This is hardly surprising when you know a little something about either Hebrew or Greek. Both the Hebrew word *ruach* and the Greek word *pneuma* can mean "breath" or "wind" or "spirit." Thus, an analogy between wind and spirit was perfectly natural; a play on words almost. What Jesus implies is that the Holy Spirit, like the wind, is invisible, and so you cannot judge where he has come from or where he is going, but you can see his effects. You can definitely see the effects on a life when someone has been born again.

I once did a revival in Garrard County in Kentucky where there was a very old man, probably older than Nicodemus, who was a new convert to Christ. He had been the small town's lothario and a heavy drinker as well. He had been befriended by one of my former students, who led him to Christ. When I met him, he was clean and sober, and filming the revival. The locals saw it as a remarkable change, not least because it happened so late in life and involved so great a change in behavior.

1. Why do you think Jesus said that more than one birth was necessary to see or enter the kingdom of God, such that even devout Jews had to be converted to do so?

2. What do you think the future kingdom on earth (as it now is in heaven) will be like?

3. Why has the Holy Spirit been called God's secret agent?

THREE

Lifted Up

John 3:9–15 *"How can this be?" Nicodemus asked. ¹⁰"You are Israel's teacher," said Jesus, "and do you not understand these things? ¹¹Very truly I* *tell you, we speak of what we know, and we testify to what we have seen, but still you people do not accept our testimony.* [12]*I have spoken to you of earthly things and you do not believe; how then will you believe if I speak of heavenly things?* [13]*No one has ever gone into heaven except the one who came from heaven—the Son of Man.* [14]*Just as Moses lifted up the snake in the wilderness, so the Son of Man must be lifted up,* [15]*that everyone who believes may have eternal life in him."*

Understanding the Word. The dialogue takes an interesting turn when an incredulous Nicodemus asks, "How can this be?" And Jesus responds, "You are Israel's teacher, and do you not understand these things?" Jesus will go on to suggest that he has been speaking of earthly things thus far, and suggests that if he were to go on to more advanced or heavenly topics, Nicodemus's credulity would be stretched to the breaking point. Interestingly, Jesus says that he speaks of things he has seen, as well as known. This suggests he is referring to some conversions that have already happened during the early days of his ministry. Notice as well that Jesus groups Nicodemus with "you people" who don't accept his testimony. Later, we learn in John 20 that Nicodemus continued to be a sympathizer with Jesus, even after his crucifixion.

Here two important points need to be made about verse 11. The first point is that Jesus punctuates his key sayings by introducing them with "Amen, amen" translated "very truly." Normally "amen" is the response of someone else to something that a teacher or prophet has said that sounds true, just as we use the word *amen* today in response to some preachers. But Jesus is amening his own teaching, affirming the truthfulness of his own testimony. This is something unique about Jesus and his style of teaching, and it tells us that he does not think his words need independent confirmation, not even "the testimony of two witnesses" as the Law suggested. Notice as well that Jesus uses only one amen in the Synoptic Gospels to introduce his key sayings, but in John it is always two. The second point is that in the Fourth Gospel there are regular references to the Jews, which in fact refers to a certain group of Jews—the Jewish leaders who frequently were doubters about the authenticity of Jesus and his teaching. Here, these same folks seem to be called "you people"—not all the people or all the Jews. The Gospel of John is not an anti-Semitic document blaming all Jews for rejecting Jesus or for his death. One has to do a careful contextual study of phrases like "the Jews" in this gospel, as the phrase is used differently in different parts.

Verse 13 brings up one of the keys to understanding Jesus in this gospel—namely, knowing where the Son of Man came from, and also where he is going. It is precisely because people do not know that Jesus came from God that they lack understanding of his identity. Thus, for example, when someone assumes Jesus ultimately comes from Nazareth, the question follows quite naturally, "How can anything good, much less messianic, come from there?" Later in this gospel, the disciples struggle to understand Jesus when he says he must go away for a while. In this gospel, the Son has come from God and will return to God, and this tells us a great deal about who he actually is.

1. Does it surprise you that Jesus suggests that the new birth is an earthly thing that Nicodemus should already understand as a teacher in Israel?

2. What do you make of the demand that even good, God-fearing people "must be born again"?

3. Do you think being born again refers to a particular kind of religious or spiritual experience, perhaps a nearly instantaneous one, or is he talking about change using a convenient metaphor?

FOUR

Love's Gift

John 3:16–18 *For God so loved the world that he gave his one and only Son, that whoever believes in him shall not perish but have eternal life. [17]For God did not send his Son into the world to condemn the world, but to save the world through him. [18]Whoever believes in him is not condemned, but whoever does not believe stands condemned already because they have not believed in the name of God's one and only Son.*

Understanding the Word. Scholars have long debated where the sayings of Jesus stop, and where the commentary of the Evangelist begins, but it seems likely that John 3:16 is the beginning of commentary by the gospel writer. But note that verse 16 is closely connected with verse 15 by the word "for," noting then the reiteration of the scope of who can be saved: in verse 15 everyone who believes in him, and in verse 16 whoever believes in him (without exception). This verse suggests that a decision of faith that we make in this life will have eternal consequences—either we will go on to everlasting life or we will perish. Notice the strong emphasis in verse 17 that Jesus did not come into this world to condemn the world, but rather to save it. Often people will ask why Jesus is said to be the only way of salvation in this very gospel. The answer is right here in this verse—namely, that Jesus is God's only begotten Son, the only one God sent to earth as a savior of humanity. No one else could do the job. There have always been many prophets, priests, and kings, but God has only sent one Savior into the world. And since Jesus' death is the one necessary and sufficient atonement for the sins of the whole world (past, present, and future), there was no reason or necessity to send other possible saviors.

Notice as well there are no neutral options—one either stands saved or condemned. And salvation requires belief in God's only begotten Son. Lest we find this unfair, it is important to remember that since the world is fallen and lost, no one is owed salvation. It is not a matter of fairness; it is a matter of grace. Justice or fairness is when we get what we deserve. And trust me: fallen humans trust me: fallen humans do not want that from a God who is both holy and just. That would be bad news. Mercy is when we have been spared our just deserts, spared the punishing for our sins. But that is not the whole story, because grace, God's unmerited favor, is when we get the positive thing we neither deserve nor have earned. Salvation is a matter of grace, not a human self-help program, and it involves both mercy on the negative side (counting not our sins against us) and pure grace (granting us everlasting life of an endlessly positive sort).

A few words need to be said about God's love. God's love is not like a heat-seeking missile, which homes in on something inherently attractive in the target audience. God's love is lavished upon us not because of what we have done, or earned, or merited, or deserved, but in spite of all these things. As John Newton, the writer of that great hymn "Amazing Grace," once said: "These two things I know, I am a great sinner, and God is a great savior." In a world where consciousness of sin is waning due to the awareness of God disappearing, many people do not realize they desperately need God; they need a Savior.

1. Why did God need to send his only Son to save the world?

2. What is the nature of God's love?

3. Why do you think so many people see God as just the giant Judge in the sky and not as the Savior?

FIVE

Final Verdict

John 3:19–21 *This is the verdict: Light has come into the world, but people loved darkness instead of light because their deeds were evil. ²⁰Everyone who does evil hates the light, and will not come into the light for fear that their deeds will be exposed. ²¹But whoever lives by the truth comes into the light, so that it may be seen plainly that what they have done has been done in the sight of God.*

Understanding the Word. This passage should be closely compared to the similar material in John 1 about light and darkness. If light means revelation, then darkness refers to the hiding of and from the truth about God, and so refers to moral as well as intellectual darkness. And here that fact is made clear. Fallen people inherently love darkness rather than light, not least because light shining in darkness exposes the darkness for what it is. One commentator graphically suggested that the situation was rather like when someone turns on the light in a basement full of bugs—they all run for cover, not wishing to be found or exposed. Maxie Dunnam once suggested that many people would prefer the familiarity of a known hell, which they have learned to endure, to the frightening prospect of having to embrace by faith a better alternative, which requires a dramatic change in their lives and lifestyles. Human beings are creatures of habit. Change, especially change that requires self-sacrifice, is indeed a bridge too far for many fallen human beings.

Have you ever noticed how people try to hide their bad behavior, or are simply in denial about it, telling lies even to themselves? And once one tells a lie to and about oneself, one eventually has to tell more lies to cover up the first one, so weaving a web around oneself that hides one from the truth, from the light. This is why our author said, "Whoever lives by the truth comes into the light"—they have nothing to fear, nothing to be afraid of, nothing to hide. There is a moral structure to the universe that ultimately favors truth and exposes lies. This is why Scripture says, "A man reaps what he sows" (Gal. 6:7). Or in other words, be sure that your sins will find you out. Blessed are those who do the deeds of light and at the end have nothing to be ashamed of, nothing to hide, but rather look forward to hearing from the Lord in the end, "Well done, good and faithful servant" (Matt. 25:21). The world is suffering from truth decay, and Jesus came to change all that. Not only did he bring the truth; he *is* the truth about humanity and God's love for us all.

1. Why do you think some people hide from or reject the offer of salvation in Christ?

2. Why is honesty and truth always the best policy?

3. What do you think causes some people to love darkness more than light?

COMMENTARY NOTES

General Comments. The Fourth Gospel has transposed a good deal of Jesus' language into a different sort of idiom. So, for example, *light* is the word used in this gospel for revelation, and *life* for salvation. In particular, "everlasting life" is a phrase used rather frequently in John, but not so much elsewhere. A key thing to bear in mind is that Jesus is talking about everlasting, not eternal, life. Strictly speaking, only God has eternal life, a life that always existed and always will exist. Everlasting life, by contrast, is a life that begins here and now with the new birth and then continues on to positive infinity, lasting forever. Thus, only in a limited and finite sense can a human being share in the eternal life of God, because of course, among other things, a human being has a definite beginning in time, and did not preexist in heaven, like God or his Son.

The unique Fourth Gospel vocabulary has various dimensions; for example, the word *kosmos* usually rightly translated "world" doesn't refer to what we might mean by cosmos—namely, the universe or space, or anywhere but this world. What cosmos means in this gospel is the world of humanity, and sometimes more specifically, the world of humanity organized against God. Thus, what John 3:16 (this most familiar of all verses) really means is that God loves even his enemies, he loves the least, the last, and the lost—he loves everyone. You will notice that John 3:16 does not say, "For God so loved the elect." No. God loved the world, even the world that hated him, all of humanity, and Jesus came and died for all of humanity, not the pre-chosen few.

Day 1, verse 3. The issue of conversion is a complex one, and it is probably a mistake to over-press the born-again or new-birth metaphor. When it comes to physical birth, the labor that leads to it can be short or long, very painful, or relatively less painful, involving a simple delivery, or a more complex one. I was once riding on a train in Egypt and a passenger told me that he had seen a woman in a field near the train working in a banana plantation in labor. She went off behind a tree, squatted, gave birth, called someone to help her cut the cord and take the baby, and then incredibly, went back to work for a while! I found this hard to take in, but it reminds us that births come in various forms and speeds and kinds. The issue with being born again is not the process or the speed, but the end result. Some people have had dramatic conversions while many have not, especially those raised in Christian families who never strayed from the church. It's not the process but the final product that matters in this case. The appropriate question is: Do you truly love the Lord, and has he changed your life?

26

Day 3, verse 14. This verse has always puzzled commentators, with its reference to Numbers 21:8–9. What sort of analogy could Jesus be drawing between the lifting up of himself on the cross, and the lifting up of the bronze serpent? The function of the bronze serpent was to protect God's people from dying of a snakebite. Those who looked on that serpent when it was lifted up on a pole lived. So the key idea here is this: if one wants to live, one must look on the one that is lifted up. This is a key theme later in this gospel when we hear things like: "when the Son is lifted up he will draw all persons to him."

Day 4, verse 16. While it is not completely clear what Jesus means by "perish" here—does he mean cease to exist? This doesn't seem to comport with what he says about Gehenna/hell and those who go there, in for example, Matthew's gospel—what is clear is that this life is the time and place of decision making in regard to how we will spend eternity.

Day 4, verses 16–18. One of the stronger contrasts in this whole passage is between believing the truth and *disobeying* the truth. Too often we have been led to think that belief is one thing (and all that is required to be saved) and behavior, more specifically obedience, is another. This very passage makes clear that this is too simplistic an analysis. Believing in the Lord is already a form of behavior, a form of obeying the command "you must believe in your heart that Jesus is Lord"

(see Rom. 10:9). Belief is not a substitute for obedience, either at the new birth or thereafter. Rather, it is the beginning of obedience of a rebellious person who has finally turned to God. This is why Jesus' brother James famously said, "Faith without works is dead," or as I would prefer to say, "Faith works." Paul spoke about "the obedience of faith" by which he does not mean that faith is a substitute for obedience. He means faith is the beginning of, and a form of, obedience. God expects not one or the other but both. We believe and we obey by means of God's enabling grace, and therefore it is never a matter of our earning our salvation. Without grace, we could neither believe nor obey God. And we need that grace every day to stay on track and in Christ. If for no other reason than that we love God, we should desire to please God, by obeying his Word.

According to the purpose statement in John 20, this gospel was written "that you may believe that Jesus is the Messiah, the Son of God" (v. 30). In a sense, then, this gospel was written for evangelists to use in sharing the good news about Jesus. And I think the church has quite naturally, if not always consciously, realized this was one of the major differences between the purpose of this gospel and the purpose of the other three canonical Gospels. The evidence of this understanding is that John has typically always been the first gospel to be translated into a new language. That is not to say that this gospel is for beginners or novices, or simply for handing out as a tract. No, there are deep waters in this gospel, and as one commentator has said, they are at the same time shallow enough for a baby to wade in, but deep enough for an elephant to drown in. This gospel is beguilingly simple in its language, but its concepts are deep and profound, and it has several levels of discourse. It is for evangelists and teachers to use with the unconverted and the newly converted, but with care, and with some simplification. This gospel allows one to plug into it at the level one is ready for. But there is always more to be discovered and deeper waters to wade into.

WEEK TWO

GATHERING DISCUSSION OUTLINE

A. Open session in prayer.

B. View video for this week's readings.

C. What general impressions and thoughts do you have after considering the video, readings, and the daily writings on these Scriptures?

D. Discuss questions based on the daily readings.

    1. **KEY OBSERVATION:** It is possible to be sincere, devout, and profoundly wrong about something, as Nicodemus was. Today, many people judge a person's faith on the basis of his or her sincerity, not on the basis of his or her fidelity to truth.

    DISCUSSION QUESTION: What do you think of this criterion for evaluating where someone is in his or her faith journey?

    2. **KEY OBSERVATION:** The new birth that Jesus speaks of is something that happens through the work of the Holy Spirit. It is not a human achievement; indeed it is not a human possibility, if by the latter we mean something we could accomplish as a self-help program. It has more to do with a transforming encounter with the divine—whether long or short, public or private, loud or quiet.

    DISCUSSION QUESTION: What do you think of the claim that unless one has had a particular kind of religious experience, one is not a genuine Christian?

3. **KEY OBSERVATION:** Scholars and laypeople alike have pondered for centuries why it was necessary for Christ to be lifted up on a cross and die a horrific death in order to save the world.

   DISCUSSION QUESTION: Why could God not simply forgive everybody and bypass the horrors of the cross?

4. **KEY OBSERVATION:** Love in the New Testament is chiefly *agape*—that is divine love— and is not a reference to human feelings, normal or exalted. This is why love can be commanded in the Old Testament and New Testament—it involves a decision of the will, worship in the heart, and obedience in actions.

   DISCUSSION QUESTION: Why do you think our world so often associates genuine love with feelings, rather than love in action?

5. **KEY OBSERVATION:** Accountability is something the Bible talks about frequently. It insists that we all shall be held accountable for the deeds we have done in the body, even if we are Christians (see 2 Cor. 5:10).

   DISCUSSION QUESTION: Why do you think so many people want truth, but without consequences, and freedom, but without accountability, not seeing that God has set up a moral universe in which, "a man reaps what he sows" (Gal. 6:7), at some juncture?

E. What facts and information presented in the commentary portion of the lesson helped you understand the weekly Scripture?

F. Close session with prayer.

WEEK THREE

John 4:3–42

Jesus Talks with a Samaritan Woman

INTRODUCTION

As with the story of Nicodemus, again the Fourth Evangelist presents an interaction of Jesus with another representative type of person he met during the course of his ministry. Instead of a pious Jew, we have an immoral Samaritan. Instead of a man who is a teacher and well respected in Israel, we have a woman who is an outcast among her own people. Instead of someone who believes in the whole Old Testament, we have a Samaritan who believes only in the Pentateuch, or the first five books of the Bible. The contrast could hardly be more stark. To understand just how stark, we need to say something about Jewish views of Samaritans.

Jews and Samaritans were not what we would call kissing cousins. Indeed, the antipathy between them was so bad that our text for this week even tells us "Jews do not associate with Samaritans," or more literally the text says, "Jews would not share a common cup with Samaritans." In ancient Near Eastern hospitality, it was normally the case that you were supposed to welcome anyone into your tent or home and be willing to break bread with them, even if they might normally be regarded as an enemy. Notice how in Psalm 23:5 we hear "You prepare a table before me in the presence of my enemies." When we hear that Jews and Samaritans wouldn't even share a glass of water with one another, you know there is some hatred involved. Jews believed that Samaritans were, at best, lapsed Jews and, at worst, immoral, unclean, recalcitrant sinners. Some early Jewish teachers said that a good Jew should never enter the unclean land of Samaria, eat with a Samaritan, or touch a Samaritan. There were nasty Jewish sayings like "The land of Samaria is like a graveyard;

it conveys a whole week's uncleanness, like a corpse" or worse, "A Samaritan woman is a menstruant from the cradle—she is perpetually unclean."

When we look at the poignant and powerful story in John 4, we should not think of it as just another story of Jesus. Read in its original context, we should ask the questions the disciples would have asked: What in the world is Jesus doing in Samaria? Why in the world is he talking with a woman he is not related to, much less a Samaritan woman? These are the kinds of questions this narrative prompts in its original context.

ONE

Oh, Well

John 4:3–9 *So he left Judea and went back once more to Galilee. ⁴Now he had to go through Samaria. ⁵So he came to a town in Samaria called Sychar, near the plot of ground Jacob had given to his son Joseph. ⁶Jacob's well was there, and Jesus, tired as he was from the journey, sat down by the well. It was about noon. ⁷When a Samaritan woman came to draw water, Jesus said to her, "Will you give me a drink?" ⁸(His disciples had gone into the town to buy food.) ⁹The Samaritan woman said to him, "You are a Jew and I am a Samaritan woman. How can you ask me for a drink?" (For Jews do not associate with Samaritans.)*

Understanding the Word. This story begins oddly, because it was not actually true that Jews had to go through Samaria when they were returning from Judea to Galilee, but Jesus chooses to here. He stops at a famous well, the well of Jacob near the town of Sychar. Since the Samaritans only believed in the Pentateuch, their spiritual heroes were the patriarchs and Moses, not David and the succeeding kings. Quite naturally, Samaritans would take umbrage at anyone who seemed to be suggesting he was greater than one of the patriarchs. This story proceeds like a slowly boiling pot, as the light gradually dawns on the woman who Jesus might really be, and then, all of sudden, she is off to announce her discovery to her townsfolk.

One of the interesting features of the Gospel of John is that no gospel more strongly emphasizes that Jesus is God the Son, and so divine. It is also true that this gospel strongly emphasizes the true humanity of Jesus as well. Thus, here we are told that Jesus is tired from his journey and obviously thirsty as well. Notice that we are told it is midday. And here is where we should ask, What's wrong with this picture?

What's wrong is that women did not come in the middle of the day to draw water from a well that is well outside town, *unless* there was a special reason. Normally women would draw water from a well or a stream first thing in the morning. So the story begins with an anomaly. Why is this woman, all by herself, coming to the well at midday? The logical explanation is that she sought to avoid contact with other women who also regularly went to this well. But why? We soon learn as the story develops.

Jesus too is alone at the well, without his disciples. They were hungry and went to town for food, leaving Jesus high and dry—especially dry in the throat. So Jesus asks the woman, "Will you give me some water to drink?"

The woman is shocked. Perhaps she had hoped to get her water and go quietly back home without talking to anyone, much less to a strange man from out of town. There were strict protocols in these cultures regarding when and to whom men and women could speak. The last thing this woman expected was to be asked for something personal, like a drink of water, which would require direct or indirect physical contact. She says, "You are a Jew and I am a Samaritan woman. How can you ask me for a drink?" This strongly suggests that Jesus' Jewishness was evident, perhaps from the clothes he wore. Possibly he has the tassels that devout Jews liked to wear. Notice that the dialogue begins on an ethnic note. This woman knows all about the ethnic tensions between Jews and Samaritans, and she was not expecting to be addressed, much less expecting a request for water. The story has a shocking opening, a shocking middle, and an equally shocking conclusion, as we shall see.

1. Why do you think the story of Jesus and the Samaritan woman has been seen as such an enduring and endearing story?

2. How does Jesus go about breaking down barriers between himself and this woman?

3. Why was Jesus' presence in Samaria in itself strange?

TWO

Thirst Quencher

John 4:10–15 *Jesus answered her, "If you knew the gift of God and who it is that asks you for a drink, you would have asked him and he would have given you living water." ¹¹"Sir," the woman said, "you have nothing to draw with and the well is deep. Where can you get this living water? ¹²Are you greater than our father Jacob, who gave us the well and drank from it himself, as did also his sons and his livestock?" ¹³Jesus answered, "Everyone who drinks this water will be thirsty again, ¹⁴but whoever drinks the water I give them will never thirst. Indeed, the water I give them will become in them a spring of water welling up to eternal life." ¹⁵The woman said to him, "Sir, give me this water so that I won't get thirsty and have to keep coming here to draw water."*

Understanding the Word. Once again, as with the Nicodemus story, there are two levels to this discourse. Jesus is speaking on one level, but the audience, both the Samaritan woman at the outset, and later the disciples, hear what he says on a much more mundane level. One of the keys to understanding this dialogue is the fact that the phrase "living water" had a very specific, almost literal meaning. It meant creek or river water, or in other words, water that was moving and so seemed to be alive. So when Jesus tells the woman he has "living water" to offer her, she thinks, *You mean to tell me that there was a creek closer to town that I could have gone to and didn't have to come all the way out to this well?*

Notice that Jesus suggests the woman needs to know "the gift of God" and "who it is that asks you for a drink." In a dry and weary land, water meant life, and it meant crops. The land of Israel had long periods during the year when there was no rain, which is exactly when this story likely takes place, between May and October. The key to understanding what Jesus means is, of course, to know who Jesus is—the big question, which is asked and answered in this gospel (see John 20:31).

The woman can be forgiven for assuming that Jesus must have been out in the sun a bit too long, and so she tells him he's got no water, nor any bucket to draw from the well. So where in the world was he going to get this moving or living water? Inquiring minds want to know. You can see that she is incredulous about the whole encounter at this point, and perhaps even a bit sarcastic. "Are you greater than our father Jacob, who gave us the well and drank from it himself, as did also his sons and his livestock?" This sounds more like a challenge than a serious question.

Jesus' response is that the water he gives is categorically different—it's the ultimate thirst quencher. One will never be thirsty again. Again, one must remember that water meant life, then as now, and here water is the metaphor for everlasting life. People can live weeks without solid food, but only a few days without water. People are thirsty for more life, and Jesus wants to give it to them, if they will only receive it. Life's not too short when it's everlasting. Jesus even suggests that once one has the gift of everlasting life, it keeps on giving, "welling up" from within and continuing to vivify the person, giving him more soul-quenching nourishment.

Sadly the woman does not yet get that Jesus is speaking to her on a non-literal, non-mundane level. At this point in the encounter, the light has not dawned, and she's still thinking about creek water!

1. Why do you think Jesus tended to speak in metaphors, and often answered questions with more questions? Was he being deliberately cryptic, or was he trying to tease the audience's minds into active thought?

2. Why is water such a good metaphor for everlasting life?

3. Why do you suppose Jacob was such an important hero figure for the Samaritans?

THREE

All Will Be Revealed

John 4:16–26 *He told her, "Go, call your husband and come back." ¹⁷"I have no husband," she replied. Jesus said to her, "You are right when you say you have no husband. ¹⁸The fact is, you have had five husbands, and the man you now have is not your husband. What you have just said is quite true." ¹⁹"Sir," the woman said, "I can see that you are a prophet. ²⁰Our ancestors worshiped* *on this mountain, but you Jews claim that the place where we must worship is in Jerusalem." ²¹ "Woman," Jesus replied, "believe me, a time is coming when you will worship the Father neither on this mountain nor in Jerusalem. ²² You Samaritans worship what you do not know; we worship what we do know, for salvation is from the Jews. ²³ Yet a time is coming and has now come when the true worshipers will worship the Father in the Spirit and in truth, for they are the kind of worshipers the Father seeks. ²⁴ God is spirit, and his worshipers must worship in the Spirit and in truth." ²⁵ The woman said, "I know that Messiah" (called Christ) "is coming. When he comes, he will explain every-thing to us." ²⁶ Then Jesus declared, "I, the one speaking to you—I am he."*

Understanding the Word. The dialogue takes a sudden left turn when Jesus, apparently out of the blue, tells the woman to go back to town, call her husband, and come back again. Her reply is honest, but does not tell the whole story. Jesus, the one who knows what is in a person's heart, says, "You are right when you say you have no husband. The fact is, you have had five husbands, and the man you now have is not your husband. What you have just said is quite true."

One can imagine the woman's eyes getting big as she blurts out, "You must be a prophet," and notice then she immediately changes the subject! This is so true to human nature. When people touch a sore spot in our lives, we don't want to talk about it, so we change the subject. And indeed, as the dialogue goes on, the story will shift from focusing on who *she* truly is, to who *he* truly is. Interestingly, she changes the subject from her own ethics to theology and the worship wars between Jews and Samaritans in regard to where was the appropriate place to truly worship the one true God. Samaritans were monotheists, but precisely because the Pentateuch was their only Scripture, they believed in one holy mountain in the holy land—not Mount Zion, but rather Mount Gerizim. The woman assumes that true worship is a matter of being on the right high place, the right mount in the right sacred zone. It is interesting that Jesus suggests to her that while the Samaritans are worshiping the right God, they don't really know who it is they are worshiping. It is a comment one might make today about other monotheists who do not know their Savior. Jesus says the reason the woman doesn't know who she worships is because "salvation is from the Jews," and more specifically, from the Jewish Messiah standing right in front of her!

Jesus says that true worship is not about finding the proper sacred space or zone, but about the way one worships—"in the Spirit, and in truth." True worship both evokes the lively presence of God himself, and it involves the conveyance of truth. It has both a cognitive and affective dimension. It is the place where head and heart are both engaged in the praise and adoration of the Maker and Savior. The main reason Jesus gives for this definition of true worship is because "God is spirit." God in the divine nature has no body, and requires no physical space like a temple in which to be kept. God cannot be confined by space or time. The character of worship is determined by the object of that worship and should agree with the character of the God who is worshiped. So it is not about sacred space, but sacred times and sacred persons.

The Samaritans did have a concept of a Messiah, but they thought he would be a prophet like Moses, based on the prophecy in Numbers 24:17–19:

> I see him, but not now; I behold him, but not near. A star will come out of Jacob; a scepter will rise out of Israel. He will crush the foreheads of Moab, the skulls of all the people of Sheth. [18]Edom will be conquered; Seir, his enemy, will be conquered, but Israel will grow strong. [19]A ruler will come out of Jacob and destroy the survivors of the city.

This star prophecy was the basis of Samaritan messianic hopes, and notice it has nothing to do with David and his descendants, only with Jacob and his offspring. Jesus, however, is prepared to say to the woman: "The one whom you are expecting has arrived, and you are talking with him now." This prompts a sudden exit, stage right.

1. Why do you think the woman changed the subject from her ethics to the more general topic of the proper place to worship?

2. What counts as true worship in Jesus' view?

3. What sort of Messiah were the Samaritans looking for?

FOUR

Food for Thought

John 4:27–38 *Just then his disciples returned and were surprised to find him talking with a woman. But no one asked, "What do you want?" or "Why* *are you talking with her?" ²⁸Then, leaving her water jar, the woman went back to the town and said to the people, ²⁹"Come, see a man who told me everything I ever did. Could this be the Messiah?" ³⁰They came out of the town and made their way toward him. ³¹Meanwhile his disciples urged him, "Rabbi, eat something." ³²But he said to them, "I have food to eat that you know nothing about." ³³Then his disciples said to each other, "Could someone have brought him food?" ³⁴"My food," said Jesus, "is to do the will of him who sent me and to finish his work. ³⁵Don't you have a saying, 'It's still four months until harvest'? I tell you, open your eyes and look at the fields! They are ripe for harvest. ³⁶Even now the one who reaps draws a wage and harvests a crop for eternal life, so that the sower and the reaper may be glad together. ³⁷Thus the saying 'One sows and another reaps' is true. ³⁸I sent you to reap what you have not worked for. Others have done the hard work, and you have reaped the benefits of their labor."*

Understanding the Word. The scene shifts now from a dialogue with the woman, to a dialogue with the disciples returning from getting their take-out lunches. As it turns out, they are about as obtuse as the woman was. She mistook what Jesus meant by water, and the disciples mistook what Jesus meant by food. Again the two-level discourse is evident, and in this case the disciples come off looking like the DUH-sciples, which is not an infrequent occurrence in the Gospels. They really look dense when they ask, "Could someone have brought him food?"

Notice that the woman is so excited she leaves her water jar at the well and runs to testify about Jesus in town. In what ensues, she and Jesus turn out to be the ones harvesting the gospel crop, whereas the disciples are just focused on feeding their faces. It's a pretty stark contrast. The woman leads many townspeople to Jesus, which one would expect was the disciples' job!

Jesus patiently explains to the disciples that what really feeds him, what really gets him out of bed in the morning, is doing the will of God and finishing the work he has been given. And obviously, part of the job is evangelizing Samaritans, no less! Jesus tells the disciples they need to open their eyes and see what a bountiful harvest is right in front of them in the persons of the Samaritans. Jesus says he has sent them to reap this harvest, but in fact someone else is doing their job—the Samaritan woman! This story is all about the reversal of expectations, and in the case of the woman, also a reversal of fortunes. She goes from being an outcast to being a follower of Jesus and one who leads others to him. The disciples nonetheless are called to rejoice in what is about to transpire, and reap the rewards of the woman's testifying.

1. What seems to be the preoccupation of the disciples in these verses? Why do you think they don't get it?

2. What does Jesus suggest his real work is?

3. Notice that at the outset of this segment, the disciples are reluctant to ask Jesus, "Why are you talking with that strange woman?" Why do you think they followed a "don't ask, don't tell" policy here?

FIVE

The Test of Testimony

John 4:39–42 *Many of the Samaritans from that town believed in him because of the woman's testimony, "He told me everything I ever did." ⁴⁰So when the Samaritans came to him, they urged him to stay with them, and he stayed two days. ⁴¹And because of his words many more became believers. ⁴²They said to the woman, "We no longer believe just because of what you said; now we have heard for ourselves, and we know that this man really is the Savior of the world."*

Understanding the Word. One of the major themes of the entire Fourth Gospel is testimony, a theme clearly reflected in the final segment of this story. The Samaritans come to faith through the sinful woman's testimony about the remarkable fact that he knew exactly who she was, and what her past was, but yet he offered her living water, everlasting life. In some ways it is no surprise that testimony figures so large in this gospel. More than the others, this is a gospel meant to aid the process of converting people, and is the only one that stresses that it goes back to an eyewitness who is giving his testimony in this narrative (see John 20–21). Jesus has suggested that his followers have the privilege not only of sowing the seed of the Word, but also of being present at the harvest when the crop comes in. Jesus believes that the eschatological age has already dawned, the age when even the least, the last, and the lost will become the most, the first, and the found. Witness exhibit A—the Samaritan woman. It can be stressed here already that a woman's testimony was not considered valid in various ancient contexts, including in courts, and yet Jesus thinks her testimony is not only valid, but vital, leading people to him. Notice the not-so-subtle put-down of the woman in verse 42—"We no longer believe just because of what you said; now we have heard for ourselves, and we know this man really is the Savior of the world."

And so excited are the Samaritans about this Jewish Savior's surprise appearance in Samaria (who would have thought it?) that they invite him to stay with them, and he and the disciples stay an additional two days. The disciples may have expected that once Jesus got food and water they could move on, and even escape enemy territory before the day was done. It was not to be. Jesus was not just passing through. He was stopping to save more lost people.

1. What was it about the woman's testimony that caused many of the Samaritans to believe in Jesus?

2. Why do you think the Samaritans urged him to stay with them?

3. What was it that led the Samaritans to know that Jesus was the Savior of the world?

COMMENTARY NOTES

General Comments. Early Jews would have seen the phrase "good Samaritan" as an oxymoron, a contradiction in terms. Samaritans and Jews had been killing each other for centuries, going back to the return from Babylonian exile in about 525 BC. The situation was very much like the relationship between Israelis and Palestinians today in the Holy Land. No typical Jew would tell a parable in which a Samaritan businessman was portrayed as a good man at the expense of priests and Levites who might have helped a Jew lying injured on the side of the road, but Jesus did. Jesus' relating to Samaritans and presenting them in a positive light was an explosive teaching in his day; it was social dynamite. The notion that Jesus was not in any way a social radical is frankly false. He was a loving, nonviolent radical, but he was definitely radical, judged by the standards of what early Judaism expected out of their teachers and holy men. He associated with the wrong people at the wrong times in the wrong ways—sinners, tax collectors, Samaritans, and women. Jewish teachers before Jesus did not have women disciples, much less Samaritan women disciples, much less immoral Samaritan women disciples— but Jesus did.

Day 1, verses 3–4. Most Jews avoided Samaria like the plague, and so when they went to a festival in Jerusalem from Galilee, they would normally cross the Jordan south of the Sea of Galilee, go down the King's Highway, recross the Jordan at Jericho, and go up the Jericho road to Jerusalem.

Day 1, verse 8. The word "disciple" actually means "learner."

Day 2, verses 11 and 15. Jesus is addressed by the Samaritan woman as *kurie*, which, technically speaking, means "lord" with a lowercase *l*, not Lord. Here it is translated "sir," the equivalent respectful normal address to a man in English. The term did not imply royalty or nobility, much less divinity. It is important to realize that Jesus, like many other respected teachers and prophets and rulers, would have been addressed as "lord" without any divine or quasi-divine implications. So for example, when in another gospel Jesus says, "Not everyone who says to me 'Lord, Lord,' will enter the kingdom of heaven" (Matt. 7:21), he is not drawing a contrast between someone who confesses he is The Lord and someone who does God's will, but rather between someone who treats Jesus with respectful addresses, but does not do what Jesus suggests he should do. Jesus is not really called Lord by others in the dialogue portions of the Gospels, not least because he did not acquire that title until he was the risen Lord. This is doubtless true to the historical realities of how Jesus was actually addressed during his ministry, before anyone really knew *fully* who he was. We must keep steadily in mind that early Jews were not looking for a divine Messiah. They just weren't. They figured the Messiah would be a son of David anointed by God's Spirit, but they didn't expect him to be the Son of God.

Day 3, verse 20. Mount Gerizim is still where the small sect of Samaritans worship today (there are only a few hundred), and interestingly, they are the only Jewish sect in the Holy Land that still offers sacrifices at Passover and performs the ancient ritual on the mountain.

Day 5, verse 31. Jesus is called rabbi, which literally means "my great one" or "my master." The Aramaic is actually *rabbouni*, and this is what Mary Magdalene calls Jesus on Easter morning in John 20. The term does not have the meaning it came to have in later post–AD 70 Judaism. It simply is a term of respect for a master teacher, not a term for an ordained, well-trained rabbi, as it would be today.

WEEK THREE

GATHERING DISCUSSION OUTLINE

A. Open session in prayer.

B. View video for this week's readings.

C. What general impressions and thoughts do you have after considering the video, readings, and the daily writings on these Scriptures?

D. Discuss questions based on the daily readings.

1. **KEY OBSERVATION:** This text confronts us with an uncomfortable situation. It deals with the importance of sharing the good news even with people who hate us, or whom we have reason to strongly dislike. In other words, it could be said to be an object lesson by Jesus as to how we should love our enemies.

   DISCUSSION QUESTION: What are some specific ways you can love your enemies?

2. **KEY OBSERVATION:** Jesus was a person who refused to make fear-based decisions in life. He was unafraid when he went into Samaria, even though he knew very well about the hatred between the Jews and the Samaritans. Making faith-based decisions as Jesus showed us can lead us into difficult places, such as a hostile land or a hostile situation. Being a good witness for Jesus even in such situations is, in fact, what we are all called to do.

   DISCUSSION QUESTION: Have you ever been faced with sharing the gospel in a difficult place? If so, how did you respond and what was the result?

3. **KEY OBSERVATION:** Jesus, without question, believed men and women were equally worthy of his teaching, as evidenced in this passage. During this time period, women were simply expected to stay home, make the food, and raise the children. Jesus, however, did not see that as their only calling in life. As we see here, the Samaritan woman went from drawing ordinary water from a well to sharing living water with her village.

   DISCUSSION QUESTION: Are there those today who seem unworthy of hearing the gospel? If so, who?

4. **KEY OBSERVATION:** Jesus does not treat either the Samaritan woman's or the disciples' mundane mistakes as things to be ridiculed or sarcastically dismissed. He invites them instead to think more deeply, probe more seriously, and get beyond the earthly things in life to the real meaning of life. Good teaching and good preaching will elevate the audience, not put them down.

   DISCUSSION QUESTION: What are some specific ways you can model Jesus' treatment of the Samaritan woman and the disciples?

5. **KEY OBSERVATION:** Jesus practices a teaching method here that fully engages his audience—the Samaritan woman—stretching her so that her reach will extend further than her current grasp.

   DISCUSSION QUESTION: Have you sat under preachers or teachers who have boiled down or oversimplified the message, rather than challenged you? How did you feel sitting under those kinds of teachings?

E. What facts and information presented in the commentary portion of the lesson help you understand the weekly Scripture?

F. Close session with prayer.

WEEK FOUR

John 9:1–41

Jesus Heals a Man Born Blind

INTRODUCTION

This, the longest story in the Fourth Gospel, is a tale of two ships passing in the night—one heading into the light, the other into darkness. There is masterful storytelling in this tale as the Jewish authorities become more and more blind, while the blind man becomes more and more seeing. In the end, it is the blind man who comes into the very presence of the Light of the World. Again we must come to grips with the two levels of discourse going on; the story is both about physical blindness and spiritual blindness, and it is both about becoming more open-hearted to Jesus and becoming more hard-hearted about Jesus. In the course of this process, the blind man grows in grace and understanding and makes more and more explicit statements about who Jesus is, which finally leads to his falling on his knees and confessing Jesus to be the Son of Man. This is the only time in the New Testament that anyone does this.

The tension in the narrative comes from several sources. On the one hand, there is the inaccurate understanding of the disciples about the relationship of sickness and sin; on the other, the inadequate understanding of the authorities about God's purposes in the Sabbath. Apparently, too, it matters whether one claims to see or not. With seeing and knowing come responsibility—if one chooses darkness rather than light, then sin raises its ugly head. The tension is also present in the scene in which the blind man is cross-examined about what happened. When he tells the authorities, his testimony simply gets him in trouble; indeed it gets him kicked out of the synagogue!

Once again, in this narrative a miracle sets things in motion, but Jesus makes no capital out of it when it comes to converting the blind man. It is simply an act of grace and mercy; the man doesn't even know who it was who heals him at the outset. He has to rely on hearsay; the miracle itself produces problems, because it is performed on the Sabbath, a day in which nothing but emergency work was supposed to be performed. Clearly, if the blind man had been blind since birth, this healing could have waited a few more hours. But Jesus deliberately chooses to go ahead with this action.

This narrative shows the skill of the storyteller, and his willingness to extend the story far longer than we find for the most part in the Synoptics. This is not a sound bite from the life of Jesus; it is a slow, simmering, complex tale that should lead to rumination, careful pondering. In other words, it is not intended as spiritual fast food for those with short attention spans.

ONE

Born Blind

John 9:1–5 *As he went along, he saw a man blind from birth. ²His disciples asked him, "Rabbi, who sinned, this man or his parents, that he was born blind?" ³"Neither this man nor his parents sinned," said Jesus, "but this happened so that the works of God might be displayed in him. ⁴As long as it is day, we must do the works of him who sent me. Night is coming, when no one can work. ⁵While I am in the world, I am the light of the world."*

Understanding the Word. The story begins abruptly. We are not told how Jesus or the disciples knew that the blind man they encounter was born blind. But the disciples make a very common assumption—namely, that sickness has been caused by some sin or malady or has been caused by someone's malfeasance. Here, and in a text like Luke 13:1–5, Jesus makes very clear that one cannot read the state of the soul from the condition of a person's body. Jesus' answer to the disciples is that this blindness was not caused either by this man's sin or his parents' sin. Jesus severs the assumed connection between sickness and sin. In a fallen world, it is not easy to tell what has led to something like blindness, and easy or pat answers are likely to be wrong. What is clear is that the man was not plagued with blindness due to sin in himself or his parents. God is off the hook here. The blind man is not a victim of blind justice. What

Jesus does say is that God will use this blindness for a good purpose. The apostle Paul said in Romans 8:28 that God can work all things together for good for those who love him. God is not the author of evil, disease, decay, or death, but he can use all things to good ends.

It is interesting that Jesus suggests several things here at the outset: 1) he has a limited time to do the work God has sent him to earth to do, so he must get on with it, even on the Sabbath. He will say elsewhere it's not as though God is idle on the Sabbath! 2) The night is coming, the night of Good Friday, and so the closer Jesus gets to the end, the more urgency there is for him to complete his mission. And 3) it makes no sense for Jesus, the Light of the World, to stand around and curse the darkness, including the blindness in this man's life, when he can do something about it in an instant. And so he does.

1. Why do you think the disciples assumed a strong connection between the man's blindness and his sin, or his parents' sin? Are there times when we see something bad happening to a person and simply assume he or she must have done something wrong?

2. What counts as work in Jesus' view? Is it appropriate to do the Lord's work on the Sabbath?

3. What ironies do you find in this whole discussion between Jesus and his disciples?

TWO

Holy Spit!

John 9:6–11 *After saying this, he spit on the ground, made some mud with the saliva, and put it on the man's eyes. ⁷"Go," he told him, "wash in the Pool of Siloam" (this word means "Sent"). So the man went and washed, and came home seeing. ⁸His neighbors and those who had formerly seen him begging asked, "Isn't this the same man who used to sit and beg?" ⁹Some claimed that he was. Others said, "No, he only looks like him." But he himself insisted, "I am the man." ¹⁰"How then were your eyes opened?" they asked. ¹¹He replied,*

"The man they call Jesus made some mud and put it on my eyes. He told me to go to Siloam and wash. So I went and washed, and then I could see."

Understanding the Word. To understand this narrative, several things need to be mentioned by way of background. It was often believed in antiquity that holy men had holy tears, holy saliva, holy sweat, holy blood, and so on. There are other stories from this era of people being healed by the saliva of a powerful person, even in one case a story about the Emperor Vespasian, retold by the Roman historian Tacitus (*Histories*, Book 4).

> Among the lower classes at Alexandria was a blind man whom everybody knew as such. One day this fellow threw himself at Vespasian's feet, imploring him with groans to heal his blindness. . . . He asked that it might please the emperor to anoint his checks and eyeballs with the water of his mouth. A second petitioner, who suffered from a withered hand, pleaded his case too. . . . At first Vespasian laughed at them and refused. When the two insisted, he hesitated. At one moment he was alarmed by the thought that he would be accused of vanity if he failed. At the next, the urgent appeals of the two victims and the flatteries of his entourage made him sanguine of success. . . . So Vespasian felt that his destiny gave him the key to every door and that nothing now defied belief. With a smiling expression and surrounded by an expectant crowd of bystanders, he did what was asked. Instantly the cripple recovered the use of his hand and the light of day dawned again upon his blind companion. Both these incidents are still vouched for by eye-witnesses, though there is now nothing to be gained by lying.

What is notable about the story is the request for healing by saliva whether we give any credence to the story or not. Now, Jesus did not need to heal using saliva or mud, but he does so to demonstrate to those observing that a healing is in process. Notice how Jesus comes down to our level to communicate in a way that the audience would readily understand. But there is another important reason as well: Jesus wants this man to participate in the process of his own healing. Hence, he is told to go and wash in the Pool of Siloam.

At first his neighbors can hardly believe that it is the same person who once was blind from birth when they see him walking around enjoying seeing the world for the first time. By now the man knows that it was someone named Jesus who healed him, but he has not yet seen him face-to-face; indeed he will not do so until the end of the narrative. The neighbors' skepticism is quite understandable since there are no Old Testament stories about sight being given to a blind person, much less a man born with no sight. *None!* Indeed there was even a Jewish tradition that said when someone comes who could do that, you would know Messiah had come. It was that rare and unexpected. Finally, notice that at the end of this segment of the story the man does not know where Jesus is, or how to find him. His spiritual journey has just begun.

1. Compare this story with the one found in John 5:1–18 about the man seeking healing in Jerusalem at a different pool—the pool of Bethesda. What similarities and differences do you notice?

2. There are several stories of Jesus giving sight to the blind in the Gospels. Why do you think it was important for the Evangelists to emphasize this kind of miracle?

3. At what juncture did the blind man gain his sight? What does this tell us about people who want to be healed, as opposed to people who would prefer the attention and pity, and even the money their illness brings to them?

THREE

Prophet and Loss

John 9:13–17 *They brought to the Pharisees the man who had been blind. ¹⁴Now the day on which Jesus had made the mud and opened the man's eyes was a Sabbath. ¹⁵Therefore the Pharisees also asked him how he had received his sight. "He put mud on my eyes," the man replied, "and I washed, and now I see." ¹⁶Some of the Pharisees said, "This man is not from God, for he does not keep the Sabbath." But others asked, "How can a sinner perform such signs?" So they were divided. ¹⁷Then they turned again to the blind man, "What have you to say about him? It was your eyes he opened." The man replied, "He is a prophet."*

Understanding the Word. We are not told who it was that brought the blind man to the authorities. Could it have been one of his nosy neighbors? We can't say. In any case, he was brought before the Pharisees, who had many extra rules about Sabbath-keeping, or better, who said extra explanations of what the Law actually required, vis-à-vis work on the Sabbath! Notice as well that no one questions the means by which Jesus performed the healing, only the day on which it happened.

It is notable that there was a division among the authorities as to how Jesus, who performed this miracle, should be evaluated, even though the healing clearly took place on the Sabbath. The question is asked, How can a sinner perform such miracles? In their view, God would not anoint or appoint a sinner to do such things. It took a holy man to perform holy miracles.

So they then ask the formerly blind man his opinion about Jesus, and here he begins to testify boldly. "He is a prophet!" says the man, presumably like other Galilean prophets who performed healings, such as Elijah. But they were not willing to let it go at that, and so the process goes on.

When we think about Jesus' many healings on the Sabbath, it becomes clear that while he would be seen as a Sabbath-breaker by many Jews, Jesus had a different view of work on the Sabbath; namely, it was the perfect day to give people release, peace, and rest from what ailed them. Jesus elsewhere calls himself the Lord of the Sabbath and says that the Sabbath was made for the good of human beings, not vice versa. The basic meaning of the word *Sabbath* is "cease," so by Jesus' logic, what better day for a man's blindness to cease! There may be one more factor in play. Jesus seems to have believed he was inaugurating the new covenant. If there is a new covenant, the old one is obsolete. It is not possible to violate a defunct law. So perhaps Jesus would have argued he did not violate the Sabbath law, because that law no longer applied now that the kingdom was breaking into this world.

1. Should Christians see the Lord's Day as their Sabbath? Why or why not?

2. What is your view of work? Should it be done on the Lord's Day?

3. Why do you think the formerly blind man suggested to his inquisitors that Jesus was a prophet?

FOUR

Passing the Buck

John 9:18–34 *They still did not believe that he had been blind and had received his sight until they sent for the man's parents.* ¹⁹*"Is this your son?" they asked. "Is this the one you say was born blind? How is it that now he can see?"* ²⁰*"We know he is our son," the parents answered, "and we know he was born blind.* ²¹*But how he can see now, or who opened his eyes, we don't know. Ask him. He is of age; he will speak for himself."* ²²*His parents said this because they were afraid of the Jewish leaders, who already had decided that anyone who acknowledged that Jesus was the Messiah would be put out of the synagogue.* ²³*That was why his parents said, "He is of age; ask him."* ²⁴*A second time they summoned the man who had been blind. "Give glory to God by telling the truth," they said. "We know this man is a sinner."* ²⁵*He replied, "Whether he is a sinner or not, I don't know. One thing I do know. I was blind but now I see!"* ²⁶*Then they asked him, "What did he do to you? How did he open your eyes?"* ²⁷*He answered, "I have told you already and you did not listen. Why do you want to hear it again? Do you want to become his disciples too?"* ²⁸*Then they hurled insults at him and said, "You are this fellow's disciple! We are disciples of Moses!* ²⁹*We know that God spoke to Moses, but as for this fellow, we don't even know where he comes from."* ³⁰*The man answered, "Now that is remarkable! You don't know where he comes from, yet he opened my eyes.* ³¹*We know that God does not listen to sinners. He listens to the godly person who does his will.* ³²*Nobody has ever heard of opening the eyes of a man born blind.* ³³*If this man were not from God, he could do nothing."* ³⁴*To this they replied, "You were steeped in sin at birth; how dare you lecture us!" And they threw him out.*

Understanding the Word. In this episode in the ongoing saga, the authorities have summoned the formerly blind man's parents, and a sordid scene ensues. The parents, afraid of the Jewish authorities and of being banned from the synagogue, practice the ancient art of passing the buck. They say only that they know the man is their son and that he was born blind, but as for the rest, since their son was a grown man, they should just stick to quizzing him!

As an aside, we are told that the Jewish authorities had already made up their minds that anyone who confessed Jesus to be the Jewish Messiah was to be given their walking papers when it came to attending synagogue. In fact, even though the man does not in fact say, "Jesus is the Messiah," they still kick him out of the synagogue. What they say is that they know Jesus is a sinner, presumably on the basis of his Sabbath behavior.

The man born blind replies that he doesn't know whether Jesus is a sinner or not (but as we shall see, he doubts it), but what he does know is that he was once blind but can now see.

The authorities don't believe his testimony. They think he is lying; they ask him a second time how he came to be healed. Finally, they accuse him of being born in sin, which presumably doesn't refer to original sin, but is rather a slur on his parents, as well as their offspring.

You can sense the exasperation of the man by verse 27 when he says, "I have told you already and you did not listen. Why do you want to hear it again?" And then in a brave moment, he says, "Do you want to become his disciples too?"

This leads to an explosion of pure polemics, where the man is falsely accused of being "this fellow's disciple" and the authorities claim to be Moses' disciples. But then comes a very telling admission—"we don't even know where that fellow comes from." Remember, knowing where Jesus came from (from God) is key in this gospel for knowing who he is. The authorities think they know who Jesus is (a sinner and a deceiver), and yet they can't say from where he came. The reason that would be pertinent to them is that if Jesus was not from Bethlehem, then he couldn't possibly be the Messiah. His point of origin would tell them all they needed to know about who the man was, except they are ignorant of this.

The incredulity of the authorities produces an equally powerful opposite reaction from the increasingly bold, formerly blind man. He retorts sarcastically (paraphrasing here), "Now that is truly remarkable! No one has ever healed a blind man like me before, and you don't even know where Jesus comes from, yet you claim to know he is a sinner. But we all know God doesn't listen to sinners, or give them healing powers, and yet here I am a living testimony that he heals people. He could do nothing if God had not empowered him and he were not from God!"

To this there is no rebuttal, only another slur on the man's character as a supposed sinner. Ironically they make the same false assumption as the disciples at the beginning of the story. Since this man was born blind, he must have been born in sin. And so the inevitable happens; he is expelled from their presence. But then the story takes another sudden right turn, as we will see next.

1. Have you ever been in a church meeting when two or more people blow up at each other? This story in John 9 would be comical if it wasn't so sad. How do you react to this uncomfortable situation?

2. Why is it important in this gospel to understand where Jesus comes from, and how should that affect the way we view his identity?

3. Can you see the spiritual growth of the formerly blind man, even in the heat of battle in this scene? What are the indicators of this growth?

FIVE

Redeemer to the Rescue

John 9:35–41 *Jesus heard that they had thrown him out, and when he found him, he said, "Do you believe in the Son of Man?"* [36]*"Who is he, sir?" the man asked. "Tell me so that I may believe in him."* [37]*Jesus said, "You have now seen him; in fact, he is the one speaking with you."* [38]*Then the man said, "Lord, I believe," and he worshiped him.* [39]*Jesus said, "For judgment I have come into this world, so that the blind will see and those who see will become blind."* [40]*Some Pharisees who were with him heard him say this and asked, "What? Are we blind too?"* [41]*Jesus said, "If you were blind, you would not be guilty of sin; but now that you claim you can see, your guilt remains."*

Understanding the Word. The formerly blind man must have been truly down and depressed after his tête-à-tête with the authorities. Normally, a person who was healed would go to the priest or the authority to get a sort of certificate of good health, and then he could return to all normal Jewish activities and synagogue. But this is the opposite of what happens to the blind man. We are told that when Jesus hears of his expulsion, he comes to the man and asks an unexpected leading question—"Do you believe in the Son of Man?" Jesus is taking the initiative to inaugurate a whole new phase in this man's life.

This is presumably the first time the man has ever seen Jesus face-to-face, and so he doesn't know either that this is Jesus, or that he is the Son of Man. Notice, however, the readiness of the man to believe: "Who is he, sir? Tell me, that I may believe in him." Here is a person who is now at the opposite end of the spectrum from those who were willfully disbelieving in Jesus. And this tells us something important: the disposition of the human heart has everything to do with what people believe. If a person is not at least open to possibilities, it is difficult for him to change his mind or embrace something new. But embracing something new is always a risk, always a step of faith. The man is prepared to trust the speaker. We are told that the man replied wholeheartedly, after Jesus indicated he was talking about himself—"Lord, I believe." The reference to worship probably refers to obeisance, the bowing down before a dignitary that one recognizes as one's superior. This is the normal meaning of the word in a Jewish mono-theistic context, when we are not talking about the worship of Yahweh.

Light can have two effects. It can illuminate a subject or bring it to light, but it can also blind a person as well. Jesus suggests that his coming into the world as the Light of the World has had both effects. He says he has come into the world so people will have to make a decision, a judgment about him. This does not contradict what John 3:16–17 says, for there the discussion is about the intention of God in sending his Son. The Pharisees thus ask, "Are we blind too?"

Jesus' response is intriguing. He says that if they were truly spiritually blind, they would not be guilty of sin in misjudging Jesus and the situation they are observing. But since they claim to be spiritually perceptive, they are responsible for their willful misjudgments of Jesus, and so their guilt remains. Notice how this whole story has focused on the issue of sin and guilt, and who is a sinner, and what counts as sin. The blind man, his parents, Jesus, the Jewish officials, all at various points in this narrative are said to be sinners of one sort or another. Only the disciples remained unscathed, but at the beginning of the story they are all wrong in their judgments about the blind man, just like the Pharisees. Things are not as they seem on the surface, and spiritual things are spiritually discerned. And so the two are heading in opposite directions—one who claims to see slipping into darkness (the Pharisees), and one who was truly blind but is coming out into the bright light of day (the blind man)—and they pass each other one last time in the presence of Jesus, the Light of the World. Only one of them is going in the right direction. This story is perhaps the most masterful narrative in the whole gospel, and it shows what an extended narrative can do to reveal the truths about the gospel and about Jesus.

1. What is it about the formerly blind man that makes him such an appealing character in this narrative?

2. Why do you think Jesus asked for a confession of himself as the Son of Man here?

3. What do you make of Jesus' suggestion that with claims of having spiritual sight and insight comes responsibility for one's judgments, and the sin and guilt that may ensue? What does this suggest to you about the care with which spiritual leaders today should approach critical evaluations of others?

COMMENTARY NOTES

General Comments. The closer one gets to the Passion narrative in the Fourth Gospel, the more stupendous the miracles become, with sign miracle number six being the narrative in John 9 (an unprecedented miracle) and the raising of Lazarus in John 11 being the climax of the whole first half of the gospel (John 1–11). This presentation has a theological purpose, and it reveals a Jesus for whom no miracle is too difficult. This is, in part, because Jesus is seen as the incarnate Son of God. But what all these miracles reveal about the world in which Jesus lived is how very needy it was, in so many different ways. People were starving (the feeding of the five thousand), were possessed by dark forces, had dread diseases that caused them to be isolated or ostracized, and were dying prematurely for all sorts of reasons. The world was a needy place, but obviously, however stupendous the miracles were, they were only temporary solutions to the human dilemma. The more fundamental problem was that death ruled the land for everyone, and many Jews did not even have a viable belief in an afterlife, whether in heaven or in the resurrection. Jesus believed that the most fundamental need of everyone was a healed relationship with God and a partaking in full salvation, which included the gift of everlasting life. In the next story, we will encounter a Jesus who is angry about and with the ravages of death, the last enemy to be eliminated.

The following are the words for salvation used in the Gospels—*sodzo* (the verb), *soter* (the noun meaning "savior"), and *soteria* (the noun meaning "salvation"). It is noteworthy that the Gospel writers are very cautious about calling Jesus a savior. This may surprise us, but this is because we don't understand the normal ancient meanings of the word. Normally, the word *saved* meant "rescued from some dire situation or condition" or it meant "healed." For example, when Jesus says to the woman with the blood flow, "Your faith has saved you," he doesn't mean she has just become a born-again Christian. She wanted healing, and Jesus is telling her it was not his magical garments but her faith reaching out to Jesus that *healed* her. Thus, it is not a big surprise that in Matthew and Mark, Jesus is not really called or addressed by the term *savior*, and even in Luke and John, it is relatively rare. The term did not usually have the later Christian sense "rescued from sin" or "born again" or some other more spiritual meaning. Normally it referred to being rescued, healed, and the like, which had a very concrete and physical meaning.

Day 2. The quotation of Tacitus from *Histories* found in today's lesson is a partial quote. What follows here is the complete quotation:

> Among the lower classes at Alexandria was a blind man whom everybody

knew as such. One day this fellow threw himself at Vespasian's feet, imploring him with groans to heal his blindness. He had been told to make this request by Serapis, the favourite god of a nation much addicted to strange beliefs. He asked that it might please the emperor to anoint his checks and eyeballs with the water of his mouth. A second petitioner, who suffered from a withered hand, pleaded his case too, also on the advice of Serapis: would Caesar tread upon him with the imperial foot? At first Vespasian laughed at them and refused. When the two insisted, he hesitated. At one moment he was alarmed by the thought that he would be accused of vanity if he failed. At the next, the urgent appeals of the two victims and the flatteries of his entourage made him sanguine of success. Finally he asked the doctors for an opinion whether blindness and atrophy of this sort were curable by human means. The doctors were eloquent on the various possibilities. The blind man's vision was not completely destroyed, and if certain impediments were removed his sight would return. The other victim's limb had been dislocated, but could be put right by correct treatment. Perhaps this was the will of the gods, they added; perhaps the emperor had been chosen to perform a miracle. Anyhow, if a

cure were effected, the credit would go to the ruler; if it failed, the poor wretches would have to bear the ridicule. So Vespasian felt that his destiny gave him the key to every door and that nothing now defied belief. With a smiling expression and surrounded by an expectant crowd of bystanders, he did what was asked. Instantly the cripple recovered the use of his hand and the light of day dawned again upon his blind companion. Both these incidents are still vouched for by eye-witnesses, though there is now nothing to be gained by lying.

The Pool of Siloam has been recently excavated by Ronny Reich, and can now be visited to give a clear image of what happened in this story and where it actually took place.

Day 4, verse 22. Various scholars have suggested that this story is actually addressing a situation much later than the time of Jesus—namely, the time of later antagonism between Jews and Christians in the late first century AD. It has been argued strongly that the reference to expulsion from the synagogue cannot possibly refer to the time of Jesus, but this ignores two important likely facts from the time of Jesus' ministry: 1) he was himself expelled from a synagogue, even his own (see Matthew 13 and Mark 6); and 2) in his commissioning of his disciples during the ministry, he warned them about rejection in various towns and told them to shake the dust off of their feet. Where would they go to share the good news of the kingdom if not to the synagogues, as well as private homes where such discussions would happen?

Thus, while this text may well have some relevance for later tensions between Jews and Christians—and may have been written with an eye on such problems, perhaps for example in Ephesus, where this gospel may have been written—nevertheless, there is nothing historically improbable about someone being expelled from a synagogue in Jesus' day. Indeed, to judge from the experiences of Paul in the Diaspora, as depicted both in 2 Corinthians 11's list of woes and in Acts, it could happen repeatedly to the same person! First Corinthians 5 suggests that Paul practiced expulsion of people from the community as well.

Day 5, verse 38. The verb *proskuneo*, found here and elsewhere in this gospel (see John 4 and the dialogue between Jesus and the Samaritan woman), has a range of meanings. At its most basic meaning it refers to bowing down or falling down at someone's feet, a gesture of submission to a superior. It can also mean to kneel or bow low, again both gestures of respect and submission. But this verb can also refer to worship, as it clearly does in the discussion about worship in John 4. In the case of John 9:38, however, it is unlikely to mean worship because: 1) Jews did not expect the Messiah to be divine. They worshiped only Yahweh. 2) Even if the man knew the verse in Daniel 7, the "one like a son of man" in that vision is distinguished from Yahweh, though he is said to be the object of worship by the nations (i.e., Gentiles). 3) This man has just now believed in the Son of Man. There has been no time to process the implications of that; belief in a person who healed you is one thing, worship another. 4) The scene in John 9 is not a worship scene. It is not in the synagogue or temple, and if indeed the man did bow down and worship Jesus, the Jewish officials would likely have been hollering, "Idolatry!" Nothing like that happens.

WEEK FOUR

GATHERING DISCUSSION OUTLINE

A. Open session in prayer.

B. View video for this week's readings.

C. What general impressions and thoughts do you have after considering the video, readings, and the daily writings on these Scriptures?

D. Discuss questions based on the daily readings.

    1. **KEY OBSERVATION:** If we compare the way the Pharisees are portrayed here with the way Nicodemus (also a Pharisee) is portrayed in chapter 3 of this gospel, we notice that the Pharisees are not always portrayed as the bad guys.

    DISCUSSION QUESTION: In what ways are you guilty of stereotyping or profiling people? What can you learn from the way Jesus views people?

    2. **KEY OBSERVATION:** In an age before modern medicine, it is hard to describe the desperation caused by having a dreadful and incurable disease or a birth defect that no one could remedy.

    DISCUSSION QUESTION: Can you imagine the desperation felt in West Africa when the incurable and dreaded Ebola virus struck and killed thousands of people?

    3. **KEY OBSERVATION:** Jesus, as a healer who could even cure previously incurable conditions, must have been in high demand, and it is not a wonder that he is depicted in various Gospels as swamped with needy people who came to be made well, and the message was seen as perhaps a bonus.

DISCUSSION QUESTION: Jesus tells his disciples that he didn't primarily come into this world to be a healer. What did he come to do?

4. **KEY OBSERVATION:** Notice in the narrative that no one questions the method by which Jesus healed the blind man (spreading mud made from his saliva on the man's eyes), but rather that he healed on the Sabbath.

   DISCUSSION QUESTION: Why do you think Jesus chose to use this method to heal the blind man?

5. **KEY OBSERVATION:** Upon meeting Jesus and learning that he is the Son of Man, the man who was formerly blind immediately believes and worships Jesus.

   DISCUSSION QUESTION: Compare/contrast this man's response to Jesus and the authorities' response to Jesus. What do their responses indicate about the human heart?

E. What facts and information presented in the commentary portion of the lesson help you understand the weekly Scripture?

F. Close session with prayer.

WEEK FIVE

John 10:1–21

The Good Shepherd and His Sheep

INTRODUCTION

Unlike much of the rest of the material in the first half of the Fourth Gospel, here we are dealing with straight teaching by Jesus and we encounter one of the famous "I am" passages. We will say more in detail about them in the following commentary notes, but here it is sufficient to note that *ego eimi* ("I am") with a predicate such as "Good Shepherd" is one thing; *ego eimi* by itself may be another. For instance, in the famous saying, "Before Abraham was born, I am" (John 8:58), there seems to be an allusion to the way God revealed who he was to Moses in Exodus ("I AM WHO I AM"—Exod. 3:14). In fact, the little phrase *ego eimi* is technically redundant—it literally means "I myself am," so the *ego* is unnecessary unless one is trying to be emphatic. Thus, in this text, Jesus is saying that *he* is the Good Shepherd. While certainly Jewish rulers and leaders were sometimes called shepherds in the Old Testament (as in Ezekiel 34), both that text and Psalm 23 make clear that Yahweh, God himself, is the shepherd of God's people. So this text, especially when one compares it to Psalm 23, suggests Jesus is making some pretty exalted claims about himself.

In this little parabolic narrative, Jesus is both the Good Shepherd and the Gate, just to mix the metaphors a bit, and his Father is the Gatekeeper. Large analogies are drawn between actual shepherding in Jesus' day and the sort of calling, guiding, and protecting of disciples that Jesus is talking about. One then needs to know something about sheep and shepherding to fully grasp the thrust of Jesus' teaching. One story will have to suffice.

Sheep are not notably bright creatures. It is not flattering when Jesus draws an analogy between sheep and his followers. Sheep need a lot of guiding and guarding, leading and loving, and sometimes the shepherd may even have to sacrifice himself for the sake of the flock. Jesus is able to introduce into this extended analogy his coming self-sacrifice for his people, really for the first time in this gospel.

Dale Carnegie grew up on a sheep farm. As a boy, his main role was to be the gatekeeper of the sheep pen, especially at the end of the day, when the sheep would be bedded down in the pen for the night. What he used to love to do was open the gate, but then put a stick into the opening, and the first sheep would jump over it to get into the pen where the food was, and the second would jump over it, and then he would withdraw the stick. And yet the third would jump, and the fourth would jump, and so on, even though the stick was not there anymore. Not notably bright animals, but they are good at playing follow the leader. We need to bear this in mind when we read this text.

ONE

Sheep-Stealing

John 10:1–2 *"Very truly I tell you Pharisees, anyone who does not enter the sheep pen by the gate, but climbs in by some other way, is a thief and a robber. ²The one who enters by the gate is the shepherd of the sheep."*

Understanding the Word. Sheep-stealing was a major problem in antiquity. It still is today in the Holy Land when it comes to Bedouin shepherds. This passage begins as a continuation of the confrontation with the Pharisees at the end of John 9. It begins with the typical "Amen, Amen" of Jesus vouching for the truthfulness of his own words, and he seems to be suggesting that the Pharisees are not merely bad shepherds, but they are guilty of sheep-stealing, hijacking God's people and leading them astray. Sheep-stealing, of course, happens today regularly in churches as well. Somebody gets the notion that he can do better than the current pastor or pastors, leads off various church members, and starts a different church. There is nothing very good or godly about such a process, as usually it involves ego and a failure to practice the Christian art of reconciliation and working through differences. And in any case, it's good to remember that sheep shifting from one church to another does not count as church growth!

Here Jesus is telling the Pharisees that they need to recognize the true shepherd, and come into the sheep pen through him, like the other sheep. Becoming a leader of God's people by some other means, avoiding the Messiah, is likened to breaking and entering, and then stealing sheep. By contrast, there is the shepherd who enters the sheep pen by the proper means—through the gate. Obviously this gets a bit convoluted since it's visually difficult to picture Jesus as both the shepherd that enters the gate, and the gate through which he enters. But the point is that Jesus is both the leader of God's people and the way into all that they need in life—leading and feeding, guiding and guarding.

1. Why do you think Jesus draws an analogy between God's people and sheep?

2. In what sense does Jesus accuse the Pharisees of illegal breaking and entering, or sheep-stealing? To what is he referring?

3. If even Jesus the Shepherd has to enter through the gate, what does this tell us about leaders who need to follow the proper procedures and rules to be good leaders?

TWO

Calling Them by Name

John 10:3–6 *"The gatekeeper opens the gate for him, and the sheep listen to his voice. He calls his own sheep by name and leads them out. ⁴When he has brought out all his own, he goes on ahead of them, and his sheep follow him because they know his voice. ⁵But they will never follow a stranger; in fact, they will run away from him because they do not recognize a stranger's voice." ⁶Jesus used this figure of speech, but the Pharisees did not understand what he was telling them.*

Understanding the Word. The teaching we find here is called a figure of speech. In other words, teaching that uses metaphors, analogies, and figurative language. Sometimes we get confused when people tell us that you must take the Bible absolutely literally if you are to have a high view of Scripture. But figurative language must be interpreted one way, and literal language another. Parables, allegories, proverbs, aphorisms, and riddles are all figures of speech. To interpret such speech correctly and properly, one *must* interpret them figuratively, not literally. For example, Jesus is not suggesting that his followers are literally growing wool on their backs, bleating, and have bad peripheral vision. He is not saying they are literally sheep. We will say more on this in the commentary notes.

It is, however, literally true that Middle Eastern shepherds do sometimes name their sheep, and then call them by name. And furthermore, sheep do recognize the sound of their shepherd's voice, not to mention the tone and intonation of the barks of the sheep dog. There comes a poignant moment in John 20, ten chapters hence, where Mary Magdalene does not recognize who the risen Jesus is in the garden until he calls her by name, and then the light dawns. Sheep are good at following the leader, and since their vision is not very good, their auditory powers compensate. They hear very well and they recognize familiar sounds. They follow the voice of their own leader, not strangers. Jesus is suggesting that the Pharisees are strangers, and that God's real sheep will not listen to them. But we are told this audience couldn't figure out Jesus' figurative language. It is probably just as well, as they would have been insulted. To them, Jesus was the stranger whose voice and command they did not recognize or respond to.

1. Why do you think Jesus so regularly spoke in figurative speech? Why didn't he just tell people plainly what he meant all the time?

2. What sort of bond ought there to be between pastors and their flock? Should the congregation blindly follow their pastor's lead? Is there a trust factor?

3. Why does Jesus lead his sheep out of the safe haven of the sheep pen and into the dangerous world? What does this tell us about how believers today should live in the world without being of the world?

THREE

Abandon Doubt, All
Ye Who Enter Here

John 10:7–10 *Therefore Jesus said again, "Very truly I tell you, I am the gate for the sheep. ⁸All who have come before me are thieves and robbers, but the sheep have not listened to them. ⁹I am the gate; whoever enters through me will be saved. They will come in and go out, and find pasture. ¹⁰The thief comes only to steal and kill and destroy; I have come that they may have life, and have it to the full."*

Understanding the Word. Jesus makes a bold claim here suggesting that before his coming God's people have been dealing with thieves, con artists, and robbers. He is not talking about Old Testament figures like Abraham or Moses, but about the immediate past history of Jewish leadership, for example, with the Herods and their allies. He would suggest the same about Annas, Caiaphas, and his offspring. In fact, both Jesus and his brother James fell afoul of the Caiaphas family, with Jesus being handed over to the Romans by Caiaphas himself, and James being executed in the early 60s by his descendant! Elsewhere Jesus called Herod Antipas "that fox" (Luke 13:32).

Jesus suggests that, thankfully, the sheep have not listened to such blind and corrupt guides and leaders. Jesus says that whoever comes through him, whatever sheep follow him, will not be fleeced, will not be slaughtered, and will not be misled. Indeed, they will be saved, or the text may mean here "kept safe," which seems more in keeping with the figurative nature of things. Under the Good Shepherd's leading, the flock get fed and led. Under the others' leading, they get taken advantage of and killed. Jesus did not come to kill the sheep, but rather to die for them. He did not come to take away their lives, but rather to strengthen them, and give them everlasting life. The picture contrasts leaders who are in it for what they can get out of it, and leaders who are self-sacrificial and put the good of the people first.

1. What models of leadership does our culture see as effective or successful?

2. Obviously, Jesus is a unique figure—the Gate, the Way of salvation—but to some degree he models for his followers what good leadership should look like. What traits do you think we might do well to emulate from this passage?

3. As for finding pasture outside the pen, what do you think this analogy is meant to suggest about the proper sources of nourishment for Jesus' followers?

FOUR

The Owner Versus the Hired Hand

John 10:11–13 *"I am the good shepherd. The good shepherd lays down his life for the sheep. ¹²The hired hand is not the shepherd and does not own the sheep. So when he sees the wolf coming, he abandons the sheep and runs away. Then the wolf attacks the flock and scatters it. ¹³The man runs away because he is a hired hand and cares nothing for the sheep."*

Understanding the Word. In an important parable in Mark 12:1–12, which comes at about the same juncture in the Markan narrative as this material does in John, Jesus suggests that the current leadership in Israel is like hired hands, or servants in the vineyard. They are not owners of the vineyard or sheep, and they know it. Indeed, in the parable of the tenants, they seek to become owners of the vineyard by killing the heir, the son of the owner who comes to demand a return from the vineyard. The real owner, the good shepherd, doesn't run in the face of danger; he protects the sheep from the wolves and, if need be, lays down his life for them in the struggle. Self-preservation characterizes the hired hand; self-sacrifice characterizes the owner. Which one really cares about the sheep and what happens to them? It is a stark portrait that Jesus paints, and we must bear in mind that it is deliberately hyperbolic. Jesus is not saying that Israel has never had good leaders, or never had self-sacrificial leaders, but he is contrasting himself with the current lot.

With ownership of something comes responsibility, and of course, caring about what happens to what you have responsibility for. It would be well to ponder why ownership changes the situation so much compared to mere employment. In this case, the phrase "lays down his life for the sheep" tells us something important. Jesus especially died for his own, in this case his own Jewish followers, and by extension, for all others who would embrace him. Jesus' death is sufficient to atone for the sins of all the world, but it is only efficient for those who accept it, and follow the Good Shepherd. It does no good to someone who does not accept the gift. The phrase "lays down his life for" implies a vicarious sacrifice—he dies *instead of others.* And perhaps we need to think more clearly about that. It should have been us on the cross paying for our sins. Indeed, Jesus is the one person for whom Jesus did not need to die, as he was not a sinner, unlike the rest of us. Mark 10:45 puts it this way: "The Son of Man did not come to be served, but to serve, and to give his life as a ransom for many" (see following commentary notes). The contrast in that saying is between the one who dies, and the many (potentially all others—see 1 Timothy 2:6), not between Jesus' death for only some and Jesus' death for all others. First Timothy 2:6 is clear—Jesus died for the sins of all people.

If one wants to be a leader like Jesus, one must give up one's right to life, liberty, and the pursuit of happiness. Inherent in the contract is self-sacrifice for others. Your life is no longer your own; you have been bought with a price.

1. What difference does it make whether one is an owner or a hired hand?

2. When Jesus speaks of wolves in sheep's clothing, whom do you think he has in mind?

3. To what degree and in what sense is looking after number one and self-preservation antithetical to the gospel, especially for Christian leaders?

FIVE

Other Sheep Not of This Fold

John 10:14–21 *"I am the good shepherd; I know my sheep and my sheep know me—*[15]*just as the Father knows me and I know the Father—and I lay down my life for the sheep.* [16]*I have other sheep that are not of this sheep pen. I must bring them also. They too will listen to my voice, and there shall be one* *flock and one shepherd.* ¹⁷*The reason my Father loves me is that I lay down my life—only to take it up again.* ¹⁸*No one takes it from me, but I lay it down of my own accord. I have authority to lay it down and authority to take it up again. This command I received from my Father.”* ¹⁹*The Jews who heard these words were again divided.* ²⁰*Many of them said, “He is demon-possessed and raving mad. Why listen to him?”* ²¹*But others said, “These are not the sayings of a man possessed by a demon. Can a demon open the eyes of the blind?”*

Understanding the Word. Many commentators have suggested that when Jesus speaks of "other sheep not of this sheep pen" he is referring to Gentiles being brought into the people of God, and certainly this is possible. But it could also be that he is referring to Diaspora Jews—Jews who have not yet heard the good news from and about Jesus. There must have been a good reason why Jesus tells the disciples during the ministry to go share the news with the lost sheep of Israel, and not to go among the Gentiles, at least initially. It is likely the same reason that we find Paul in Acts going first to the synagogue in place after place as he evangelizes the largely Gentile world; and it is why in Romans 1 Paul says the good news is for the Jew first (and he was the apostle to the Gentiles!). Notice that Jesus makes clear as well that whoever these other sheep are, he himself must bring them. It is wise for all of us to remember that only Jesus is the Savior, the true Good Shepherd. Ministers should not develop savior complexes. We are rather like one beggar showing another beggar where the bread is, but we didn't bake the bread that nourishes unto everlasting life. Jesus is the true Evangelist of all the sheep, and eventually they must hear and follow his voice on their own if they are to be saved.

In the final segment of the passage, Jesus makes some astounding claims: 1) that no one takes his life from him without his permission; indeed he insists that he will freely lay it down; and 2) that he will take it back up again (though elsewhere in the New Testament we hear that God the Father or the Spirit raised him from the dead).

In verse 19, once again the phrase "the Jews" probably refers to the Jewish leaders, who are said to be divided about Jesus. Some think he has a demon, and others say he couldn't have cured the blind man if that were the case. They will be less divided after Jesus raises Lazarus from the dead in next week's scripture. It is interesting that Jesus also says here that one of the reasons God the Father loves him is that he obeys the Father, and freely lays down his life for the sheep. God's love may be unconditional, but its expression is often prompted by what we say and do.

1. Why do you think Jesus told the disciples to go to the lost sheep of Israel first before going to the Gentiles?

2. In this passage, Jesus claims that he will take his life back up again. Read Acts 4:8–10 and Romans 8:11. In these verses, who raised Jesus from the dead?

3. We notice here that the Jews were divided about Jesus. What kinds of division about Jesus do you see today?

COMMENTARY NOTES

General Comments. There are quite a lot of "I am" sayings in the Fourth Gospel, none of which we find in the Synoptics. Scholars have sometimes, therefore, been skeptical that these sayings actually go back to the historical Jesus, but it is possible that what we have in this gospel is the mode in which Jesus taught when he was in Judea rather than Galilee. Notice that we also have none of the parables found in the Synoptics in this gospel, while we do have figurative or metaphorical teachings, like in John 10. This seems deliberate, and so most scholars think that the Fourth Evangelist knew at least the book of Mark, and chose to write a different sort of gospel, not simply treading all the same ground covered in the earlier gospels. I think this is likely correct. The Synoptics present us with the Galilean Jesus and his Galilean followers, the Fourth Gospel focuses more on Judea and the unique teachings and miracles performed in that region.

As for the "I am" sayings themselves, here is a helpful list:

John 6:35, 48: I am the bread of life.
John 8:12; 9:5: I am the light of the world.
John 8:58: Before Abraham was, I am.
John 10:9: I am the gate.
John 10:11: I am the good shepherd.
John 11:25: I am the resurrection and the life.
John 14:6: I am the way and the truth and the life.
John 15:1: I am the true vine.

Notice that one of these sayings is not like the others—namely, John 8:58. All the other sayings have predicates and involve figurative speech. John 8:58 is a claim not about Jesus' roles or attributes or functions, but about his preexistence. He existed in heaven before Abraham. In a culture that believes the older is the better, and the earlier more primary, and the more senior person the one who has more authority, this is an important statement. Biblical cultures were not fixated on youth, but rather, they revered the older and wiser ones, which is why the leaders in each community were called elders. They tended to be elderly! In the world of the Bible, a religion was judged to be genuine if it had long stood the test of time. This is why the Romans recognized Judaism as a legitimate religion, and allowed Jews to practice it. But when it became clear that Christianity was a new religion, it fell into the category of superstition or something about which to be suspicious. The newer was not seen as the truer, and the latest was not seen as the greatest in Jesus' world, unlike ours.

Notice as well that these sayings are found in both the Book of Signs (John 1–11) and the Book of Glory (John 12–20). They help bind the two halves of this gospel together. These "I am" sayings with a predicate reflect Jewish Wisdom teaching about the things wisdom could give a person (see Proverbs 8–9). Jesus then is seen as the quintessential expression of Jewish

Wisdom, giving all the things wisdom had merely offered—leading and feeding, guiding and guarding. Finally, notice that the two sayings in the middle of the list are overview or summary statements; Jesus is the resurrection and the life, and Jesus is the way, the truth, and the life. In short, it's one-stop shopping in Jesus when it comes to revelation, inspiration, salvation, sanctification, glorification, life, learning, and so forth.

The Greek word *paroimia* here (John 10:6; see also 16:29) is different from the word *parabole*, and it is the former that is used here and elsewhere in the Fourth Gospel. The two terms have a certain overlap in a sense, but the Synoptics use the latter, while the author of John uses the former, and there are some differences. Thus, properly speaking, there is nothing like the Synoptic parables in the Fourth Gospel; extended metaphors and figures of speech about Jesus, such as the "I am" sayings in John, yes; parables of the kingdom, no.

Day 4. Many Bible translations and versions translate Mark 10:45 as, "and to give his life as a ransom *for* many." The Greek preposition used here is *anti*. While "for" is a proper translation, this may also be translated "instead of." The phrase "laying down his life for" implies a vicarious sacrifice—he dies *instead of others.*

WEEK FIVE

GATHERING DISCUSSION OUTLINE

A. Open session in prayer.

B. View video for this week's readings.

C. What general impressions and thoughts do you have after considering the video, readings, and the daily writings on these Scriptures?

D. Discuss questions based on the daily readings.

1. **KEY OBSERVATION:** One can sense the rising tide of opposition to Jesus the closer we get to Passover Week, and this is especially apparent in John 9–11.

   DISCUSSION QUESTION: What is Jesus' response to the opposition?

2. **KEY OBSERVATION:** To really appreciate passages in the Bible, it is important to know something about antiquity. As I like to say to my students, a text without a context is just a pretext for what you want it to mean. The Bible must be studied in context.

   DISCUSSION QUESTION: How has understanding shepherding in antiquity, and understanding sheep in general, helped you to understand what Jesus is saying in this week's passage?

3. **KEY OBSERVATION:** One of the major motifs of this gospel is that Jesus is in charge. Nothing happens to him without his permission, nothing by pure accident The sovereignty of Jesus over his own life and its circumstances is made very clear in this gospel.

DISCUSSION QUESTION: How does understanding the sovereignty of Jesus over his life and circumstances affect the way you see Jesus' death on the cross?

4. **KEY OBSERVATION:** Jesus is the very revelation, the incarnation of the Father. If you want to know what God is really like, look at Jesus, because as Jesus says, he and the Father are one. He is the spitting image of his Father, such that the one who has seen the Son has seen the Father.

   DISCUSSION QUESTION: What attributes of Jesus, and thus the Father, do you see in this week's pericope?

5. **KEY OBSERVATION:** Jesus chose to compare God's people to sheep. Sheep don't clean themselves like cats, they don't lavish attention on their owners like dogs, they aren't beasts of burden on which one can lay heavy loads, and they can't readily find their own food or water.

   DISCUSSION QUESTION: Why, in a world full of animals, do you think Jesus picked sheep as the image for God's people?

E. What facts and information presented in the commentary portion of the lesson help you understand the weekly Scripture?

F. Close session with prayer.

WEEK SIX

John 11:1–57

Lazarus Raised from the Dead

INTRODUCTION

The Book of Signs finishes with a stupendous miracle that turns out to be the straw that breaks the camel's back, a miracle that leads to the plot against Jesus, and the desire to arrest him, lest his following grow any further. John 11, however, is nowhere to be found in the Synoptics. Those writers seem to know nothing of this narrative; indeed they know nothing of Lazarus at all. True, we hear about an encounter between Jesus and Mary and Martha in Luke 10:38–42 when Jesus visits them in Bethany. But there is no mention of Lazarus in that story, or anywhere else in the Synoptics (the Lazarus in the parable of the rich man and Lazarus is clearly depicted as someone else; see Luke 16:19–31).

In fact, in the narrative outline in this gospel there is no preparation for this story before John 11. We do not hear of these three siblings before now, and so it comes as something of a surprise that we are told in John 11:3 that Lazarus is "the one you love." This statement is important because before this remark, no one in this gospel has been so identified. There has been no reference at all to a Beloved Disciple, and for the first-time listener who is listening to the gospel story in its original order, this reference to "the one you love" followed by further references to a particular individual called the Beloved Disciple, would have normally and naturally led to the conclusion that Lazarus is the Beloved Disciple. Going forward through the second half of the gospel, we will see how this makes the best sense of the further references to the Beloved Disciple in this gospel.

The important thing to know going into the reading of this story is that even Jews who believed in a positive concept of an afterlife by means of resurrection also believed that the spirit of the deceased person left the corpse by the fourth day. Thus, in the view of those present when Jesus arrived, Lazarus was past hope or help, even from Jesus. Decay and rot had already set in, with the usual bad smell, and all of this is why Martha, who certainly does believe in Jesus, nonetheless suggests he shouldn't open the tomb!

Mourning in a Jewish context usually went on for a week, so it is not a surprise to find mourners, including Jewish officials from Jerusalem, still around on day four after Lazarus died. Finally, while we call this man Lazarus, his actual biblical name was Eliezer, like the other Lazarus in Luke 16.

ONE

A Dire Situation

John 11:1–16 *Now a man named Lazarus was sick. He was from Bethany, the village of Mary and her sister Martha. ²(This Mary, whose brother Lazarus now lay sick, was the same one who poured perfume on the Lord and wiped his feet with her hair.) ³So the sisters sent word to Jesus, "Lord, the one you love is sick." ⁴When he heard this, Jesus said, "This sickness will not end in death. No, it is for God's glory so that God's Son may be glorified through it." ⁵Now Jesus loved Martha and her sister and Lazarus. ⁶So when he heard that Lazarus was sick, he stayed where he was two more days, ⁷and then he said to his disciples, "Let us go back to Judea."*

⁸"But Rabbi," they said, "a short while ago the Jews there tried to stone you, and yet you are going back?" ⁹Jesus answered, "Are there not twelve hours of daylight? Anyone who walks in the daytime will not stumble, for they see by this world's light. ¹⁰It is when a person walks at night that they stumble, for they have no light." ¹¹After he had said this, he went on to tell them, "Our friend Lazarus has fallen asleep; but I am going there to wake him up." ¹²His disciples replied, "Lord, if he sleeps, he will get better." ¹³Jesus had been speaking of his death, but his disciples thought he meant natural sleep. ¹⁴So then he told them plainly, "Lazarus is dead, ¹⁵and for your sake I am glad I was not there, so that you may believe. But let us go to him."

¹⁶*Then Thomas (also known as Didymus) said to the rest of the disciples, "Let us also go, that we may die with him."*

Understanding the Word. This story begins with introducing us to Lazarus for the first time. It is very interesting indeed that the Evangelist identifies Lazarus's sister by means of a story he was not going to tell until later in John 12! We must remember that these stories were oral traditions passed along for a long period of time before they found their way into this written source, and so the Evangelist is simply reminding his audience which Mary he was referring to in this case. We are in fact told in verse 5 that Jesus loved this whole Judean family. And precisely because of this, his behavior upon hearing the news seems exceedingly odd. It appears that Jesus is going to wait to go to Bethany until the man has died! Lest we see this as an example of Jesus' lacking compassion, we must bear in mind that Jesus can raise the dead, and that throughout this gospel, Jesus has to wait for the go-ahead from the Father before doing things, and that is probably the case here.

Was Jesus a false prophet when he said, "This sickness will not end in death" and then Lazarus went on to die? As it turns out, the answer is no. Jesus will go on to speak of Lazarus's death using the euphemism of sleep, which was not uncommon in early Judaism as a way to refer to the dead. The term was used by those who believed in the resurrection, believing that death was no more permanent than sleep, something that one could come back from alive by means of the resurrection. Jesus is not suggesting that death is like sleep in its nature. He doesn't believe we will be snoozing in the afterlife. He is suggesting only that the condition is temporary, and that God will use the death of Lazarus as an occasion for Jesus' glory to shine forth.

Thus it is that Jesus waits two more days and then says to his disciples, "Let us go back to Judea." The disciples, nervous Nellies that they often are, counsel against this move in light of a previous attempt to stone Jesus there. Jesus' response to this warning is cryptic, but the gist of what he is saying is that he must do the will of the Father, the work of ministry while it is still day, while there is still time to get some things accomplished. Jesus knows he is on the clock, and it is ticking and "night is coming when no one can work" (John 9:4). So he needs to get on with it, especially when it involves some of his own loved ones.

The exchange between Jesus and the disciples makes us wonder who was really asleep during this whole process. The disciples fail to understand that Jesus means Lazarus is dead and he is going to remedy the situation. Jesus then has to spell it out for them. Notice that Jesus calls Lazarus "our friend" (*philos*), assuming perhaps the disciples have a prior relationship with him as well.

This section closes with a revealing look at Thomas (Didymus means "the twin," but the twin of whom?), who in fatalistic-sounding suggestion says, "Let us also go, that we may die with him." Here Thomas seems to be depicted as Mr. Doom and Gloom. Later, in John 20 he is depicted not merely as doubting Thomas, but as lacking faith, as we shall see.

1. What strikes you as odd about the beginning of this story that climaxes the first half of this gospel?

2. What is the significance of the phrase "the one you love" in 11:3, in light of subsequent references to a disciple whom Jesus loved?

3. How can God use a loved one's death for displaying his glory?

TWO

Martha Confronts Jesus

John 11:17–27 *On his arrival, Jesus found that Lazarus had already been in the tomb for four days. . . . [20]When Martha heard that Jesus was coming, she went out to meet him, but Mary stayed at home. [21]"Lord," Martha said to Jesus, "if you had been here, my brother would not have died. [22]But I know that even now God will give you whatever you ask." [23]Jesus said to her, "Your brother will rise again." [24]Martha answered, "I know he will rise again in the resurrection at the last day." [25]Jesus said to her, "I am the resurrection and the life. The one who believes in me will live, even though they die; [26]and whoever lives by believing in me will never die. Do you believe this?" [27]"Yes, Lord," she replied, "I believe that you are the Messiah, the Son of God, who is to come into the world."*

Understanding the Word. Martha is clearly depicted in both Luke 10:38–42 and here as the more outgoing of the two sisters, and so naturally she is the first one to go out and meet Jesus as he approaches their home in Bethany. Bethany was indeed only a couple of miles from the heart of Jerusalem, and it may well be that this was Jesus' home base when he was in Judea, just as Capernaum at the house of Peter's mother-in-law was his home base when he was in Galilee. We hear from the outset that many Jews (which again may refer especially to Jewish officials) had come to mourn with the family during the week of mourning.

While Martha's grief must be taken into account, it is hard not to hear her opening remarks to Jesus as something of a rebuke. Martha knows Jesus' power to heal, and she is bitterly disappointed Jesus wasn't there to help. She adds however, "But I know that even now God will give you whatever you ask." She is not thinking of immediate resurrection from the dead, as the continuing dialogue makes clear, so it is not clear what she means by this remark.

Jesus tells her that her brother will rise again. She acknowledges the belief in the traditional Jewish idea that there will be a corporate resurrection of believers at the Last Day, whenever it may arrive. Jesus does not simply affirm this belief; he trumps it by saying not merely that can he give resurrection (even now), but that he *is* the Resurrection. Whoever comes into contact with Jesus, the life source, whatever their condition—well or ill, alive or dead—can be made truly alive. It needs to be made clear that this kind of claim goes well beyond what was expected of the coming Messiah, or a great prophet. They might say that by the power of God, healing could come through them, but they would not say *I am life.*

Jesus will use the term "die" in a couple of senses in his response to Martha. He says, on the one hand, that even if a person dies he will live again if he has believed in Jesus. But then he goes beyond this to say that a person who believes in him will avoid eternal death altogether. Notice the words "whoever lives by believing in me will never die." It may be some such saying as this that led to the later belief that once Jesus raised Lazarus, the Beloved Disciple, from the dead, that he would never physically die again. This would explain the conundrum of John 21:22–23, where the Evangelist feels he must explain that Jesus did not say that the Beloved Disciple would live until his second coming, but only "if it is my will that he do so." The audience would not need this disclaimer if the Beloved Disciple had not in fact died again. While I am not an archaeologist, nor do I play one on TV, I would love to find the tombstone of Lazarus—it would say "died AD 29" and then below that "died again AD 87" (or whatever). This would confuse some scholars who do not believe in resurrection of the dead. Notice that resurrection here is not seen as automatic at the end times but specifically predicated on the basis of faith in Jesus.

Jesus then asks Martha, "Do you believe this?" Again, her response is true, but inadequate. She affirms that he is the Jewish Messiah and the Son of God, but notice she doesn't say, "You are the Resurrection and the Life." She interprets what Jesus says in the context of her preexisting Jewish messianic beliefs. As we have noted before, there is a crescendo of confessions in this gospel, confessions that are true about Jesus, but not fully adequate, until, ironically, unbelieving Thomas gets in the last word, confessing Jesus to be Lord and God, which matches up with the prologue in John 1. Those disciples were certainly unpredictable.

1. What do you make of Martha's confrontation of Jesus and then her confession?

2. How close a relationship do you think Jesus had with this family, whom he seems to know intimately?

3. What are the differences between the resurrection of Lazarus and the resurrection of Jesus?

THREE

Mary, Did You Know?

John 11:28–37 *After she had said this, she went back and called her sister Mary aside. "The Teacher is here," she said, "and is asking for you." . . . ³⁰Now Jesus had not yet entered the village, but was still at the place where Martha had met him. ³¹When the Jews who had been with Mary in the house, comforting her, noticed how quickly she got up and went out, they followed her, supposing she was going* *to the tomb to mourn there.* ³²*When Mary reached the place where Jesus was and saw him, she fell at his feet and said, "Lord, if you had been here, my brother would not have died."* ³³*When Jesus saw her weeping, and the Jews who had come along with her also weeping, he was deeply moved in spirit and troubled.* ³⁴*"Where have you laid him?" he asked. "Come and see, Lord," they replied.* ³⁵*Jesus wept.* ³⁶*Then the Jews said, "See how he loved him!"* ³⁷*But some of them said, "Could not he who opened the eyes of the blind man have kept this man from dying?"*

Understanding the Word. The encounter between Jesus and Mary seems even more emotional than the encounter with Martha. Mary comes with the very same thing on her mind and her lips as her sister—if only Jesus had been there before Lazarus died. And so she verbally repeats the same lament, word for word! One wonders if they were twin sisters. Jesus does not lead Mary through a process of enlightenment, but seeing that she is weeping, and that her Jewish fellow mourners were weeping, the text says, "He was deeply moved in spirit, and troubled."

Verse 33 has frequently been misinterpreted, and here the knowledge of Greek itself is essential. The key verb here to express Jesus' emotional response to the tears is *embrimaomai* and invariably it has the sense of anger, even outrage, or indignation when it is predicated of a human being. The grief and weeping of Jesus comes from anger and the translation "moved with indignation" (TLB) is more nearly right than what we have above from the New International Version. When predicated of an animal it refers to the angry snorting of a horse before it rears or charges.

But anger at what? Since we know that this response is to the tears of Mary and the Jews, the most natural way to read this is that Jesus is upset at the lack of faith in him who is the Resurrection. These people were mourning like those who had no hope for Lazarus's immediate future. Thus, when the Jews are moved to say, "See how he loved him!" as Jesus himself begins to weep, there is an irony in the words. For while they were right that Jesus loved Lazarus, that is not what he is crying about. Verse 37 confirms the above interpretation, for it suggests that the Jews think of Jesus as impotent in the face of death, though he was able to cure the blind man. In other words, this passage is not mainly about Jesus' compassion on those he loved, though that is implied. His tears and deep emotions come from the lack of understanding of who he is and what he can do. While verse 35 is indeed the shortest verse in the New Testament, it is also one of the most misinterpreted. Jesus wept over the lack of faith in him. But as we shall see in verse 38, Jesus isn't finished being upset yet.

1. How does Jesus' response to Mary differ from his response to Martha, even though they have the same identical complaint?

2. How does knowledge of the Greek prevent misinterpretations of a text like verses 33–35?

3. Some people seem to think that being angry is un-Christian. What does the example of Jesus in this story and in the temple-cleansing episode suggest to you about that matter?

FOUR
An Heir-Raising Incident

John 11:38–44 *Jesus, once more deeply moved, came to the tomb. It was a cave with a stone laid across the entrance. ³⁹"Take away the stone," he said. "But, Lord," said Martha, the sister of the dead man, "by this time there is a bad odor, for he has been there four days." ⁴⁰Then Jesus said, "Did I not tell you that if you believe, you will see the glory of God?" ⁴¹So they took away the stone. Then Jesus looked up and said, "Father, I thank you that you have heard me. ⁴²I knew that you always hear me, but I said this for the benefit of the people standing here, that they may believe that you sent me." ⁴³When he had said this, Jesus called in a loud voice, "Lazarus, come out!" ⁴⁴The dead man came out, his hands and feet wrapped with strips of linen, and a cloth around his face. Jesus said to them, "Take off the grave clothes and let him go."*

Understanding the Word. Verse 38 uses the same Greek word as verse 33, which indicates that Jesus is deeply disturbed (see also John 12:27; 13:21 for the same verb). Here Jesus' anger could be at the ravages of death, or it could be at the lack of faith even after all the miracles he had already performed.

In response to Jesus' command to take away the stone from the tomb, Martha suggests not to since there would be a big stink. Jesus' response can only be said to be testy, and probably should be punctuated with an exclamation point: "Did I not tell you that if you believe, you will see the glory of God?" Once again believing is said to lead to seeing and understanding, not the other way around. Miracles can confirm a preexisting faith. They can unsettle unbelief. They can lead to the wrong sort of faith (a faith in the shaman who performs healings on demand).

What Jesus most fervently wants in this situation is that the people might believe that he is the sent Son of God. Notice as well when he speaks about the Father always hearing him. This suggests that he is praying for the miracle to happen, trusting his Father for it. Jesus has clear channel reception from and to God the Father.

Jesus then cries out in a loud voice: "Lazarus, come out!" Notice he addresses the corpse as a person, a deceased person, but nonetheless, still a person who can be addressed even in death. Lazarus does come, and Jesus instructs them by all means to unwrap the present!

1. Are you surprised that Jesus could get angry, even with people he loved? Why do you suppose unbelief angered him so much?

2. What do you think Jesus means here by seeing the glory of God?

3. Why would Jews have been reluctant to take the winding sheet off of Lazarus? What would they have been afraid of?

FIVE

The Plot Thickens and Sickens

John 11:45–57 *Therefore many of the Jews who had come to visit Mary, and had seen what Jesus did, believed in him.* [46]*But some of them went to the Pharisees and told them what Jesus had done.* [47]*Then the chief priests and the Pharisees called a meeting of the Sanhedrin. "What are we accomplishing?" they asked. "Here is this man performing many signs.* [48]*If we let him go on like this, everyone will believe in him, and then the Romans will come* *and take away both our temple and our nation." ⁴⁹Then one of them, named Caiaphas, who was high priest that year, spoke up, "You know nothing at all! ⁵⁰You do not realize that it is better for you that one man die for the people than that the whole nation perish." ⁵¹He did not say this on his own, but as high priest that year he prophesied that Jesus would die for the Jewish nation, ⁵²and not only for that nation but also for the scattered children of God, to bring them together and make them one. ⁵³So from that day on they plotted to take his life. ⁵⁴Therefore Jesus no longer moved about publicly among the people of Judea. Instead he withdrew to a region near the wilderness, to a village called Ephraim, where he stayed with his disciples. ⁵⁵When it was almost time for the Jewish Passover, many went up from the country to Jerusalem for their ceremonial cleansing before the Passover. ⁵⁶They kept looking for Jesus, and as they stood in the temple courts they asked one another, "What do you think? Isn't he coming to the festival at all?" ⁵⁷But the chief priests and the Pharisees had given orders that anyone who found out where Jesus was should report it so that they might arrest him.*

Understanding the Word. The response to this stupendous miracle is mixed. On one hand, some began to believe in Jesus (though what exactly they believed about him is not said). On the other, some went and reported him to the authorities, and this prompted a crisis meeting of the Sanhedrin. Things had gone too far, and right under their noses, just outside of the city limits of Jerusalem.

There is the complaint that whatever actions they had taken to keep Jesus in check thus far, it had accomplished nothing. And then they express their living nightmare—that if they couldn't control their own people, then the heavy-handed Romans might take even more direct control over their temple and their nation. Caiaphas responds that it would be expedient for that one man to die, so the nation might be spared further and even worse nightmares of occupation. Interestingly, the Evangelist takes this remark to be an unintentional prophecy of what was going to actually happen, and he adds the comment that Jesus would die not only for the Jewish nation, but for all the scattered children of God as well, so that they might all be one. Again we see irony in the narrative. The very person who wants to do away with Jesus prophesies how he will do away with evil and the effects of sin. Caiaphas was indeed a cynical, sarcastic, self-serving man, and this is how the Jewish historian Josephus portrays the Sadducean leaders of the people in general (*Wars* 2.166). Thus the plot to do away with Jesus was hatched.

But Caiaphas was not the only prophet in town. Jesus knew what was coming and retreated to Ephraim, near the Judean wilderness. And he does not return immediately when the festival begins, and people begin to ask for him. He will, however, return to Jerusalem for a special celebration in Bethany—to dine with Lazarus and his family now made whole.

1. What do you think many of the Jews believed about Jesus?

2. What is ironic about the statement made by Caiaphas in verses 49–50?

3. What was it about Jesus that so upset the members of the Sanhedrin?

COMMENTARY NOTES

General Comments. As we have seen, to really understand a complex text like this, an exact knowledge of what the Greek says can prevent all kinds of misreading of a passage. Every translation is already an interpretation, even the most literal ones, because the translators have to decide the meaning of words in specific contexts. Words do not have meaning in isolation. It is not true that in the beginning was the dictionary. Dictionaries are simply repositories of detailed studies of how words are used and what their meanings are in diverse contexts. For example, the word *row* in English can mean: 1) a verbal command to take the oars and make the boat move; 2) a noun referring to a line of seats or something else; or 3) a noun referring to a ruckus or melee. We need to bear in mind that the original inspired Word of God was written not in English, but in Hebrew, Aramaic, and Greek. The closer to the original source, the closer to the original sense.

There is something very odd about this whole situation in Bethany. Why exactly do we have three grown children living together without parents or spouses? How had this happened? And why exactly does Lazarus die prematurely? Here we may have a clue from the parallel account in Mark 14 to the story in John 12. We are told there that the anointing, which is said in John 12 to happen in the house of Mary, Martha, and Lazarus, happens in the house of Simon the leper.

Now the light dawns. Leprosy (Hansen's disease) certainly existed in Jesus' world, and it was contagious. If indeed the family had been infected and affected by this dreaded skin-eating disease, and if the father of Simon had already died, and now the son had died prematurely, it is entirely understandable why no one would marry these children! They may have lived in an isolated house at the edge of town, and people would only come around when duty truly called, such as at a funeral. But there is more to ponder.

Notice that in the story in Luke 10:38–42, while the story opens by saying Jesus is with the disciples, it then adds that Martha only opens her house to Jesus! He alone has the dialogue with Mary and Martha on that occasion. Apparently, the disciples stay outside. Also, in John 11, notice that neither Jesus nor the disciples enter the house of Lazarus before he is raised from the dead. After that miracle, perhaps the message got through that the disciples need not worry about leprosy as long as Jesus, the resurrection and the life, was around!

There is one further crucial bit of contextual material one needs in order to understand this text. Basically, only men could inherit major property. Women could have a dowry, but could not inherit property. This is what makes a story like the widow of Nain's son in Luke 7 or this story in John 11 so poignant and disturbing. These women were likely about to lose not only the man in their family but their property and livelihood as well! The property would go to the next nearest male kin in the larger extended family. This explains a further urgent need for Jesus' actions if life was going to go on as normal in these families.

We have seen in this story just how precious this family of Mary, Martha, and Lazarus was to Jesus. They are his friends, and even more than that, Jesus is said to love Lazarus dearly. Of no one else in John 1–11 is that said. It would appear then that the Evangelist is telling us— "If you have eyes to see, you will realize that the Beloved Disciple is the one Jesus raised from the dead." And that brings up one final point.

There have always been conjectures as to why this gospel is so very different from the Synoptics. One possible answer is staring us in the face—if someone raises you from the dead, that will quickly change your whole worldview! Perhaps this gospel is the one that was written entirely through the eyes of resurrection faith, whereas the others were written by people who had not literally experienced resurrection yet. Perhaps that's why John 11 is the end of the Book of Signs, and directly parallels the story about the resurrection of Jesus at the end of the Book of Glory, in John 20. The story of the one whom Jesus loved climaxes the first half of the gospel, and the Beloved Disciple returns the favor by making the story of the one who the Beloved Disciple loved the climax of the rest of the story. It's worth a thought.

WEEK SIX

GATHERING DISCUSSION OUTLINE

A. Open session in prayer.

B. View video for this week's readings.

C. What general impressions and thoughts do you have after considering the video, readings, and the daily writings on these Scriptures?

D. Discuss questions based on the daily readings.

   1. **KEY OBSERVATION:** Irony is when someone says more than he or she realizes, or says one thing and actually means another, or the wrong person says the right thing, and so on. This gospel is literally filled with irony.

   DISCUSSION QUESTION: What irony do you see in this passage?

   2. **KEY OBSERVATION:** What people do in a crisis, and what they say in a crisis, often reveals a lot about their character.

   DISCUSSION QUESTION: What do you learn about the character of the two sisters and the character of the disciples in this story?

   3. **KEY OBSERVATION:** None of the resurrections that transpired before the resurrection of Jesus were the same as that of Jesus.

   DISCUSSION QUESTION: What was different about the resurrection of Lazarus compared to the resurrection of Jesus?

4. **KEY OBSERVATION:** In John 11, we have reached the climax of the seven sign narratives; if there is one thing we should have learned it is this—people cannot be impressed into believing. There is a certain ambiguity to what belief means when we hear about believing after a miracle happens.

   DISCUSSION QUESTION: In this passage, what do the different characters believe about Jesus?

5. **KEY OBSERVATION:** In John 11:3, we are told that Lazarus is "the one whom [Jesus] loves."

   DISCUSSION QUESTION: Have you ever considered Lazarus to be "the disciple whom Jesus loved" referred to in John 20:2? What are your thoughts about this?

E. What facts and information presented in the commentary portion of the lesson help you understand the weekly Scripture?

F. Close session with prayer.

WEEK SEVEN

John 12:1–36

Jesus' Triumphal Entry into Jerusalem

INTRODUCTION

John 12 can be called a transitional chapter providing the seam that stitches the Book of Signs in John 1–11 to the Book of Glory, which really begins with the second story in this chapter, the triumphal entry of Jesus into Jerusalem. John 12:1–11 looks back to John 11, and shows us the sequel to that remarkable story, transpiring some time later when Jesus returned to Bethany from Ephraim. If this story can be called the Return of the Friend, the next one is the Return of the King.

Notice how the very first verse of the chapter tells us once more that Lazarus lived in Bethany, because in fact these stories were originally separate oral traditions, only later woven together into a seamless narrative account.

As we have already mentioned, John 12 has a clear parallel in the Synoptics, in Mark 14:3–9 but also in Matthew 26:6–13. The latter likely draws on the Markan account, and the Johannine account appears to be independent of the Markan and Matthean accounts. We must focus on the Johannine telling of the story, but it should be noted that it is more substantial than the Synoptic parallels. Mary is named as the anointer, and Judas as the complainer about the waste of money. We are told in John that this event transpired six days before the Passover, so presumably early in Passover Week. While in John this event is mentioned before the triumphal entry, in Mark and Matthew it is well after that momentous entry on a donkey. It is right to suspect that the Fourth Evangelist has placed this passage here for theological and narrative reasons: to bind the two halves of this gospel together and to provide a context for understanding the meal that follows in John 13, where we have the foot-washing story, found only in John.

ONE

A Prophetic Anointing

John 12:1–11 *Six days before the Passover, Jesus came to Bethany, where Lazarus lived, whom Jesus had raised from the dead. ²Here a dinner was given in Jesus' honor. Martha served, while Lazarus was among those reclining at the table with him. ³Then Mary took about a pint of pure nard, an expensive perfume; she poured it on Jesus' feet and wiped his feet with her hair. And the house was filled with the fragrance of the perfume. ⁴But one of his disciples, Judas Iscariot, who was later to betray him, objected, ⁵"Why wasn't this perfume sold and the money given to the poor? It was worth a year's wages." ⁶He did not say this because he cared about the poor but because he was a thief; as keeper of the money bag, he used to help himself to what was put into it. ⁷"Leave her alone," Jesus replied. "It was intended that she should save this perfume for the day of my burial. ⁸You will always have the poor among you, but you will not always have me." ⁹Meanwhile a large crowd of Jews found out that Jesus was there and came, not only because of him but also to see Lazarus, whom he had raised from the dead. ¹⁰So the chief priests made plans to kill Lazarus as well, ¹¹for on account of him many of the Jews were going over to Jesus and believing in him.*

Understanding the Word. We are told that the meal depicted in John 12 is given in honor of Jesus, doubtless because of what he had recently done for the family. We are told more specifically that while Martha serves (see Luke 10), Lazarus reclines with Jesus. This was the normal protocol. The head of the household would recline on a couch with the chief guest. It is important to compare John 12:2 with John 13:23, where we are told that Jesus is again reclining with a particular person, there said to be the Beloved Disciple. Now for those who were simply listening to John 11–John 13 in sequence, the normal or reasonable conclusion to draw would be that here we have chronicled two meals, each involving Lazarus and Jesus reclining on the same couch. It is not impossible that John 13:23 refers to someone else as the Beloved Disciple but in light of John 11:1–3, one would have expected further explanation if someone other than Lazarus was meant. But no such explanation is forthcoming in John 13, and furthermore, nothing is said in John 13 about the sharing of a Passover meal either. And by the same token, nothing is said in the Synoptics about Jesus washing feet at the Last Supper. I would suggest that this is because the meal recorded in John 13 transpired earlier in Passover Week, just like the one in John 12. In fact, John 13:1 says rather generically that the meal transpired "before the Passover Festival." Not during Passover or as a Passover meal, but before the entire festival. This explains as well why there is no reinterpretation of the Passover elements in John 13—no "this is my body, this is my blood." In fact, the Gospel of John no more records the Last Supper than it records the Transfiguration. It chooses other events to record. We will say more about John 13 in next week's sessions.

Having sorted that out, we need to concentrate on the extravagant act of love performed by Mary—she pours a whole pint of nard on Jesus! No wonder the Markan account says it smelled up the whole house! In John she pours the nard on Jesus' feet (in the Synoptics on the head, but with that much quantity used it could easily have been both). In any case, we are told that this much nard cost a whole year's wages of a day laborer—three hundred denarii. The focus here is on the anointing of the feet, perhaps because Jesus is going to interpret this act as a memorial like one would perform at the burial of a person. He interprets it in terms of his coming death, regardless of what would have been the intent of Mary, which we are not told.

Judas immediately objects, saying it's a big waste, and the money could have gone to the poor. Here we have a negative editorial remark, not only that Judas would later betray Jesus, but that Judas was crass and didn't really care about the poor. He was a thief who loved money. This does comport with the thirty pieces of silver story as well. We also learn that he was the treasurer of the Twelve, and not reluctant to dip into the communal funds for his own purposes.

Jesus responds to Judas sternly, telling him to back off and let her "keep" or "observe" it, as she wouldn't have the occasion to use it when Jesus was actually buried, so this could be interpreted as a prophetic burial act. It will be remembered that Jesus was buried in haste, as both Sabbath and Passover were coming quickly and the sun was going down. The female disciples who did see where he was laid had no time to pay their respects with the linens and the oils and spices, and neither would Mary have been able to do so.

Jesus' famous saying about "the poor you will always have with you" should certainly not be taken as some sort of cynical remark, justifying the neglect of the needs of the poor. Jesus himself had on numerous occasions attended to such needs, and could never have implied that. What he was saying was that this was a special occasion and he would only be around for a while longer, and so it was appropriate. There would always be more times to help the poor.

The passage closes with a remark about people coming to gawk at Lazarus, because they had heard he had been raised from the dead, which precipitated a further frantic plan of the authorities to do away with Lazarus as well. Of course this is profoundly ironic, because if God could raise Lazarus once, he could raise him twice! Killing Jesus or Lazarus was not going to stop God's will for either of their lives, as it turns out.

1. When you compare the three accounts in Mark, Matthew, and John of the anointing, what similarities and differences do you note?

2. Did you note the irony in the Markan account, which fails to give Mary's name, but suggests she will be remembered forever wherever the gospel is told?

3. What we make of Judas and his actions during the last week of Jesus' life is important, right up to and including his own suicide. Do you think Jesus would have had the same forgiveness for Judas as he had for Peter or even the bandit on the cross?

TWO

When Love Comes to Town

John 12:12–19 *The next day the great crowd that had come for the festival heard that Jesus was on his way to Jerusalem. *[13]*They took palm branches and went out to meet him, shouting, "Hosanna!" "Blessed is he who comes in the name of the Lord!" "Blessed is the king of Israel!" *[14]*Jesus found a young donkey and sat on it, as it is written: *[15]*"Do not be afraid, Daughter Zion; see, your king is coming, seated on a donkey's colt." *[16]*At first his disciples did not understand all this. Only after Jesus was glorified did they realize that these* *things had been written about him and that these things had been done to him. ¹⁷Now the crowd that was with him when he called Lazarus from the tomb and raised him from the dead continued to spread the word. ¹⁸Many people, because they had heard that he had performed this sign, went out to meet him. ¹⁹So the Pharisees said to one another, "See, this is getting us nowhere. Look how the whole world has gone after him!"*

Understanding the Word. The presentation of the triumphal entry in John 12 is more succinct than some of the Synoptic accounts. In the Synoptics we are told that two disciples are sent to find Jesus a colt or donkey to ride on, and we are further told they had just come to Bethany. Now, this should ring some bells. It is very unlikely that they would have gone randomly and said to just anyone that the Master had need of it, but if they went to Bethany and knocked at Lazarus's door, they would get a ready reception, and it would be known immediately who the Master in question was. We are told quite specifically in Mark that Jesus said, "Go to the village ahead of you and ask." Comparing the two stories with one another makes better sense of both of them. In John we are not told about the requisitioning of the animal.

What we are told about is palm branches, not mentioned directly as palm branches in Mark (there it says branches from in the fields, which could mean all kinds of things). Again, the Johannine account is more circumstantial and specific. Some scholars have said there were no palm trees in Jerusalem at this time, which may be true. It doesn't really matter because palm branches were readily available in Jericho, and the Galilean pilgrims would mostly have gone through there and up the Jericho road. Palm branches were the symbols used to celebrate the Maccabean victory, retaking Jerusalem during the Maccabean wars. Waving them was quite specifically a symbol of military victories, and it may well have signaled what the crowds thought of Jesus getting on a donkey and riding into town like a king.

This is the only occasion in the entire ministry of Jesus where he intentionally elevates himself above the crowds. The Evangelist relates the story to Zechariah's peaceable king, and Zechariah 9:9 is appropriately quoted. Jesus is even called the King of Israel in this presentation. The exclamations "Hosanna!" and "Blessed is he who comes in the name of the Lord!" were regular pilgrimage sayings, part of the psalms of ascents in Psalms 120–34, which were the regular road songs of the pilgrims as they sung their way up to Jerusalem.

In verse 16, we have a clear admission that the disciples did not understand all these things, and indeed it was only after the crucifixion, resurrection, and ascension that the light truly dawned and they began to see how the Scriptures had been fulfilled in Jesus, particularly during the last week of Jesus' life. Again we should note verses 17–18, where these events are specifically related to John 11; the news about Jesus' spectacular raising of Lazarus was spreading by those who had seen it or heard about it and the crowds were going out to meet Jesus on this occasion, giving the Pharisees more heartburn and apoplexy.

1. Why do you think Jesus picked a donkey, rather than, say, a warhorse?

2. Take a moment to read Zechariah 9. How was Jesus living into this prophecy?

3. What did the palm branches signal? Do you think it would have made the authorities even more nervous when palm-branch waving accompanied riding into town on a donkey like a king?

THREE
The Greeks Come Calling

John 12:20–26 *Now there were some Greeks among those who went up to worship at the festival. ²¹They came to Philip, who was from Bethsaida in Galilee, with a request. "Sir," they said, "we would like to see Jesus." ²²Philip went to tell Andrew; Andrew and Philip in turn told Jesus. ²³Jesus replied, "The hour has come for the Son of Man to be glorified. ²⁴Very truly I tell you, unless a kernel of wheat falls to the ground and dies, it remains only a single seed. But if it dies, it produces many seeds. ²⁵Anyone who loves their life will lose it, while anyone who hates their life in this world will keep it for eternal life. ²⁶Whoever serves me must follow me; and where I am, my servant also will be. My Father will honor the one who serves me."*

Understanding the Word. It is probably a mistake to see the Greeks here as a reference to pagans. Pagans would not come to worship in Jerusalem at Passover.

More than likely, we are talking about Greek-speaking Jews, perhaps from the Diaspora, but there was a synagogue for the Hellenists in Jerusalem (i.e., for Greek-speaking Jews living in Jerusalem), and this may have been some of them. Why would they approach someone like Philip? Well, he has a Greek name of course, and may have spoken Greek. Bethsaida was a border town in Galilee, and there would have been a regular need for Greek by the fishermen selling their wares to all sorts of people, including Gentiles living in and around Galilee. It is interesting, however, that it is in this gospel at John 1:44 and here that Philip and Andrew gain some prominent mention. You will notice that in the Fourth Gospel, people come and seek out Jesus. He doesn't so much call disciples in this gospel as he attracts them by word of mouth and a sort of spiritual gravity. As we have mentioned before, the gospel writer is concerned about presenting all kinds of different people seeking out Jesus (remember Nicodemus, the Samaritan woman, and so on). This is quite deliberate, as the author sees Jesus as the Savior of the world, and especially of God's people everywhere.

At verse 23, Jesus announces that his hour has come, the hour when he is to be glorified. But what he means by that is glorification of an odd sort—by being lifted up on the cross. No one in antiquity, so far as we can tell, saw crucifixion as a noble way to die. It was, rather, the most shameful way to die. But Jesus changed all that. Notice that here Jesus calls himself the Son of Man, just as he earlier referred to the Son of Man descending from heaven, or he urged the blind man to confess that Jesus was the Son of Man. This is not because he is emphasizing his humanity, but because he is suggesting he is the figure referred to in Daniel 7:13–14. He is the one God has sent to judge the world, be worshiped by the world, and rule the world forever. That vision portrays a person who is both human, and yet more than human. Jews would not worship a mere mortal, not even their Messiah. So there is an exalted claim when Jesus says the Son of Man will be glorified.

Jesus then warns that anyone who would follow him must be prepared to die for the sake of the cause. It may seem paradoxical, but Jesus says that those who love their present lives and try to preserve them will lose them, whereas those who are prepared to sacrifice themselves will gain everlasting life, and the heavenly Father will honor them. It is like the missionary Jim Elliot once said not long before he was martyred by one of those he was evangelizing: "He is no fool who gives what he cannot keep [i.e., this life] to gain what he cannot lose [i.e., everlasting life]."

1. Who were the Greeks and why did they want to see Jesus?

2. What does Jesus mean by "his hour"?

3. Why did Jesus mainly identify himself as the Son of Man, referring to himself in the third person?

FOUR

A Voice from on High

John 12:27–33 *"Now my soul is troubled, and what shall I say? 'Father, save me from this hour'? No, it was for this very reason I came to this hour.* *²⁸Father, glorify your name!" Then a voice came from heaven, "I have glorified it, and will glorify it again." ²⁹The crowd that was there and heard it said it had thundered; others said an angel had spoken to him. ³⁰Jesus said, "This voice was for your benefit, not mine. ³¹Now is the time for judgment on this world; now the prince of this world will be driven out. ³²And I, when I am lifted up from the earth, will draw all people to myself." ³³He said this to show the kind of death he was going to die.*

Understanding the Word. The alert reader will have noticed that not only do we have no actual Passover meal recorded in the Fourth Gospel (no proper Last Supper with words of institution about a new covenant), but we also have no Garden of Gethsemane agony either. What we seem to have instead is this little vignette in John 12 where Jesus is deeply troubled in his soul; he prays and receives a word from on high. This word involves, among other things, a voice from heaven, which some interpret as thunder and others as an angel speaking, but Jesus heard loud and clear what was said—namely, "I have glorified it, and will glorify it again."

Among the many things that were true about Jesus, he was also a seer, a person who has visions from heaven, who hears and sees things others mostly can't hear and see. So for instance, at his baptism in Mark 1, the sky cracks and he hears God speaking to him and sees the Spirit descending like a dove on him. Or in the wilderness he has a vision of Satan in which he sees the pinnacle of the temple and the whole world, but actually he was still just in the Judean wilderness when he had this vision. Elsewhere Jesus says to his disciples, "I saw Satan fall like lightning from heaven" (Luke 10:18). In other words, from time to time Jesus had visions and auditory revelations from above, much like John of Patmos in the book of Revelation. This should not surprise us, and it can help us understand this text. Jesus is receiving assurance from above that he is following the plan and things are on schedule. His hour is at hand, and he does not wish to be saved from it, but he wants others to be saved by it.

But what he is talking about is a redemptive judgment. If that sounds like an oxymoron, a contradiction in terms, it is not. Satan, the hidden ruler or prince of this world, and his minions must be judged so that his captives can be freed, in order for salvation to come to one and all, and in order for Jesus to draw all people to himself. Jesus refers to his being lifted up as the means of this liberation. The prince of this world could not have seen this one coming. He would have liked nothing more than to do away with Jesus in the most shameful way possible. But God had a plan to use the crucifixion to judge the powers of darkness and set the world free from them. Paradoxical it was; a contradiction in terms, it was not.

1. What does it mean to say Jesus was a visionary?

2. Why do you think we do not have the Garden of Gethsemane agony scene and the sleeping disciples in John's presentation?

3. In what sense was Jesus' revelation from heaven objective, and in what sense subjective? Did others get the message as well?

FIVE

Crowd Control

John 12:34–36 *The crowd spoke up, "We have heard from the Law that the Messiah will remain forever, so how can you say, 'The Son of Man must be lifted up'? Who is this 'Son of Man'?" *[35]*Then Jesus told them, "You are going to have the light just a little while longer. Walk while you have the light, before darkness overtakes you. Whoever walks in the dark does not know where* *they are going. ³⁶Believe in the light while you have the light, so that you may become children of light." When he had finished speaking, Jesus left and hid himself from them.*

Understanding the Word. There is not much interchange between Jesus and crowds in the Synoptics, but there is a bit more in John, and here is one of the instances. Notice that we are told that the crowd spoke up and quoted Scripture; this reflects the collective group as a whole, though doubtless some individual or individuals did the talking. Their claim that the Law said that the Messiah will remain forever may seem odd. The Pentateuch doesn't say that anywhere. The term *Law* is probably a cipher for the whole of the Old Testament; Torah would more likely have been the term originally used. But what text anywhere in the Old Testament could be meant? I would propose it is surely Daniel 7:13–14, which does indeed suggest that this messianic figure will rule forever. The inquisitors seem to have taken that to mean that Messiah would never die. Thus, with that assumption, it wouldn't make sense that the Messiah was going to be lifted up, if that had anything to do with death. Did it rather mean he would be taken up into heaven? But if so, why then does Daniel suggest he would rule forever on earth? These are precisely the kinds of debates, based on interesting interpretations of the Old Testament, that one might have expected between Jesus and various religious officials, so it is rather ironic that here it is the crowd that raises the question.

Notice, however, that Jesus doesn't answer the question "Who is this 'Son of Man'?" In fact, he does not directly answer any of the questions here, stated or implied. Rather, Jesus warns them that the light is waning and they need to be walking in it, before the darkness descends, just as Jesus must work in the light before night comes. What is required is that they actually believe in the light that Jesus is shedding and sharing, the light that Jesus *is*, which enlightens all (see John 1). Believing is required if one is going to become a child of light. One does not have that by some birthright. It needs to be kept steadily in view that from the very beginning of this gospel we have been told that no one is born a child of God! No indeed, "Yet to all who did receive him, to those who believed in his name, he gave the right to become children of God—children not born of natural descent, nor of human decision, or of a husband's will, but born of God" (John 1:12–13). The story of Nicodemus in John 3 simply expands on this theme.

This section ends with Jesus hiding himself from the crowd. This comports with the earlier word that Jesus, knowing what is in the hearts of people, would not deliver himself into their hands (John 2:24).

1. Why do you think the crowd asked Jesus this particular question about the Messiah?

2. The crowd asks "Who is this 'Son of Man'?" Do you suppose they were making a connection between Jesus and "this 'Son of Man'"?

3. Why didn't Jesus answer the questions, and why did he run off and hide?

COMMENTARY NOTES

General Comments, Day 1. Dining at special meals in early Judaism involved reclining on couches, just as was the custom in the Greco-Roman world. So we must immediately get out of our minds all those pictures of the Last Supper with thirteen people all sitting at a table! Instead they would have reclined on various separate couches usually a couple of people to a couch. In the case of Jesus, we must envision his feet not underneath some table, but rather, hanging off of the end or back of the couch. The anointing then is far easier than it would be if Mary had to crawl under a table!

There were various sorts and purposes to anointing in antiquity, and various substances used for the purpose. Normal olive oil was regularly used to anoint hands, feet, and head when a person came off the hot, dusty roads in Israel (see Luke 7:36–50). It was a regular part of hospitality, and Jesus missed it when it was not offered by the host, in this case Simon the Pharisee. There was also the sacral anointing of prophets, priests, and kings; these were normally on the head alone, and might involve olive oil, but it might also involve something aromatic, like nard. Pistic nard was a popular but expensive perfume used for anointing. We must also bear in mind that perfume was used in lieu of deodorant, and so women regularly wore small phials of perfume around their neck to mask the body odor in a hot country. Finally, there was also the anointing of

corpses, and this involved both oil and spices of various sorts (usually myrrh was one of the main ones). The spices were meant to retard the odor, especially during the week or so when the mourning would happen and the body might be visited. Mary uses the expensive pistic nard on Jesus, hence the outcry of Judas.

Judas's other name, Iscariot, has been interpreted in various ways. It has been suggested it means "man of Kerioth," in which case he may have been the only Judean disciple among the Twelve. It could simply be patronymic indicating whose son Judas was. But more intriguingly it could mean "one of the *sicarri.*" Now, the *sicarri* were the hit men among the Zealots. They were supportive of the violent overthrow of the overlords, including the Roman ones and those who cooperated with them (tax collectors, priests, etc.). It is quite possible that Judas, perhaps especially after the triumphal entry and temple cleansing, had hoped Jesus would indeed be a son of David like David himself, and lead an armed revolt against authorities. If he truly hoped this, then Jesus dashed his hopes by explaining he had come to Jerusalem to die, not to kill. This would have crushed zealotic hopes about Jesus, and may have been what led to Judas betraying Jesus, thinking he was a false Messiah.

Day 4. John 12:27–33 can meaningfully be compared to other visionary experiences in the New Testament, for instance the threefold account of Paul's vision of Christ on the Damascus Road in Acts 9, 22, and 26. I say this because we notice that Paul is the recipient of the communication, but others know something objective is happening, though all they hear is a sound and all they see is a light. However, Paul sees Jesus and hears his audible voice. The same is true in John 12. Visions from God are not purely subjective in nature. They come from outside a person, though of course they are received within that person. Real visions are not examples of an overheated imagination or dreams. Neither Jesus nor Paul was a mere dreamer, but each did have visions from time to time. Second Corinthians 12:1–10 recounts one of Paul's visions, and we have already mentioned several of Jesus' visions. God can communicate in many different ways, and visions are one of them.

WEEK SEVEN

GATHERING DISCUSSION OUTLINE

A. Open session in prayer.

B. View video for this week's readings.

C. What general impressions and thoughts do you have after considering the video, readings, and the daily writings on these Scriptures?

D. Discuss questions based on the daily readings.

1. **KEY OBSERVATION:** There is an interesting variety of stories in John 12, and they do not flow together like some of the longer continuous narratives in this gospel.

    DISCUSSION QUESTION: Why do you think the Evangelist arranged the stories in John 12 as he did?

2. **KEY OBSERVATION:** Passover was the most popular of all the Jewish festivals, sometimes attracting several hundred thousand people. This is when Jesus cleanses the temple and rides into town on a donkey.

    DISCUSSION QUESTION: Was Jesus riding into town on a donkey the kind of king the crowd was expecting? Why or why not?

3. **KEY OBSERVATION:** Judas is one of the more interesting characters in this gospel. To some he will seem rather like Darth Vader, to others a terribly misguided Zealot, and to still others a greedy, selfish individual who, when he couldn't have a messiah like he wanted, decided to betray the one of whom he had been a disciple.

DISCUSSION QUESTION: What is your impression of Judas?

4. **KEY OBSERVATION:** During this festival season, what should have been endless celebrations of Passover, of the exodus events, and of liberation from bondage, there was a very dark undercurrent caused by the controversial actions and teachings of Jesus, which had rattled the cages of various religious groups and authority figures.

   DISCUSSION QUESTION: What was it about Jesus that upset the various religious groups and authority figures?

5. **KEY OBSERVATION:** If we are to understand the world in which Jesus lived, we need especially to understand that this was an honor-and-shame culture. By that I mean that one of the highest values in that culture was obtaining honor and avoiding shame.

   DISCUSSION QUESTION: What do you see in this passage that indicates that this was an honor-and-shame culture?

E. What facts and information presented in the commentary portion of the lesson help you understand the weekly Scripture?

F. Close session with prayer.

WEEK EIGHT

John 13:1–38

The Last Supper

INTRODUCTION

We have already noticed the creativity of the Fourth Evangelist in arranging his material. He was also skilled at combining materials to bring out the points he wanted to make. We will see this vividly illustrated in John 13:31–17:26, the so-called Farewell Discourses, that combine the teaching Jesus offered on several different occasions during Passover Week. John 13:1–30 in itself seems to be a further illustration of this skill. It appears that our gospel writer has combined the story of two meals that Jesus shared with his disciples the last week of his life: one that took place as John 13:1 says, before the real beginning of the Passover festival and involved a foot washing, and another which took place on Thursday night of Passover Week, the meal we call the Last Supper.

It is as important to notice the unique things included in this chapter (the foot-washing episode) and the things that are left out (the reinterpretation of the Passover bread and wine as the body and blood of Jesus). It is difficult to know why these editorial decisions were made, especially if the writer did indeed know Mark's gospel, which says nothing about the foot washing, and focuses on the reinterpretation of the Passover meal. But perhaps it was precisely to fill in the gaps in Jesus' last week of life, telling the stories the previous Evangelists had not told. And there may be one further reason as well. One of these meals at least involved the Beloved Disciple, who is the source of the unique materials in this gospel, indeed whom we are told in John 21 wrote down his memoirs and is the basis of the vast majority of this gospel.

What needs also to be stressed is that there is a purpose to the arrangement of all of John 13–17, which leads up to the Passion events themselves beginning in John 18. Our Evangelist has put together a sequence of meals followed by discourses, which is exactly what normally happened in an ancient Greco-Roman–style meal in antiquity. There would be a meal, attended by family and friends, and then afterward there would be a *synposion* (a Greek word from which we get the word *symposium*). This was the after-dinner time, when there would be a speaker—a philosopher, a rhetorician, a teacher—and those present would listen to the discourse while drinking their final cups of wine. Since the Fourth Gospel was likely written in Ephesus, a large pagan city, and since this gospel was meant to be a tool to aid followers of Jesus in converting those in the city, we can now see why the Evangelist might well shape these stories in John 13–17 about Jesus to make them immediately more usable for those doing the evangelism in that city.

ONE

Prime Time

John 13:1–5 *It was just before the Passover Festival. Jesus knew that the hour had come for him to leave this world and go to the Father. Having loved his own who were in the world, he loved them to the end. ²The evening meal was in progress, and the devil had already prompted Judas, the son of Simon Iscariot, to betray Jesus. ³Jesus knew that the Father had put all things under his power, and that he had come from God and was returning to God; ⁴so he got up from the meal, took off his outer clothing, and wrapped a towel around his waist. ⁵After that, he poured water into a basin and began to wash his disciples' feet, drying them with the towel that was wrapped around him.*

Understanding the Word. According to the Johannine chronology, the meals depicted in this chapter all took place before the slaughtering of the lambs and the proper celebration of Passover, which would have begun at sundown Friday evening with the Sabbath coinciding with the celebrating of the Passover meal. It is possible, perhaps likely, that Jesus instigated an early celebration of Passover on Thursday night, but in none of the gospel accounts of that meal is there any mention of the main attraction—the lamb itself. Some have suggested, especially in John, where Jesus is overtly proclaimed the Passover Lamb (John 1:36), that the writers wanted the focus on Jesus as the Passover, rather than on the meal as the Passover. This is probably correct. In the Fourth Gospel we do not even have the words of reinterpretation of the bread and the wine, unless we see the verses in the bread of life discourse in John 6:53–56 as the foreshadowing or a repositioned example of those words:

> "Very truly I tell you, unless you eat the flesh of the Son of Man and drink his blood, you have no life in you. ⁵⁴Whoever eats my flesh and drinks my blood has eternal life, and I will raise them up at the last day. ⁵⁵For my flesh is real food and my blood is real drink. ⁵⁶Whoever eats my flesh and drinks my blood remains in me, and I in them."

This first paragraph of this chapter focuses on Jesus' knowing what time it is and what he must now do. He must prepare to leave the world, and return to his Father in heaven. There is a vertical dimension to the Christology in this gospel (the Son is the one who has come down from heaven and must go back where he came from), which, coupled with the lack of emphasis on the return of Christ to earth, gives this gospel a very different feel than the Synoptics. The Synoptics seem very linear—everything pushing forward toward the eschaton and the return of the Son of Man. This paragraph illustrates this orientation.

The second part of the long first sentence in the Greek here is of particular interest: "having loved his own who were in the world, he loved them *eis telos.*" This probably means unto the end of his life, rather than as some translations have it "to the full extent." The context is about the end of his life, and so this is likely correct.

The dark shadow invades the proceedings already at verse 2, where we are told that the devil had already goaded Judas into planning to betray Jesus. While Judas is now in the dark, in the clutches of the dark lord, Jesus is not in the dark about what is about to happen. While the devil had put the suggestion into the mind of Judas, the Father had put all power into the hands of Jesus. He would lay down his life. No one would snatch it from him.

Jesus then, with one last large symbolic gesture, intends to demonstrate to his disciples what real leadership looks like—it is servant leadership. And so Jesus takes on the demeanor and task of a slave, stripping himself down to his undergarments, wrapping a towel around him, and taking a basin of water, and going from couch to couch, washing the feet of the disciples who must have been stunned by this gesture, and felt awkward. Peter not surprisingly vocalizes this very thing.

I know just how they felt. I was once asked to preach in a Church of the Brethren service in Ashland, Ohio. The Brethren tradition involves foot washing with the Lord's Supper every time it is celebrated, done in the context of a fellowship meal. After I preached in the sanctuary upstairs and we had finished the regular service, we all proceeded downstairs for the meal and the celebration. When we got to the Lord's Supper, all of a sudden I had a senior citizen taking my shoes and socks off, and preparing to wash my feet! My instinctive reaction (being a good Methodist, who had never had an experience like this before) was to say just about what Peter said: "No way should you be doing this for me; I should be doing it for you!"

1. When you knew something was inevitable in your life, and you needed to prepare for that eventuality (e.g., an upcoming birth of a child), was your focus on yourself, or was it more like Jesus'—directed toward others?

2. What do you think of Jesus acting like a slave in this story? Does this fit with your understanding of who he was?

3. Foot washing is a humbling experience. Why do you think more Christian churches don't follow this practice?

TWO

Peter Puts His Foot in His Mouth

John 13:6–11 *He came to Simon Peter, who said to him, "Lord, are you going to wash my feet?" ⁷Jesus replied, "You do not realize now what I am doing, but later you will understand." ⁸"No," said Peter, "you shall never wash* *my feet." Jesus answered, "Unless I wash you, you have no part with me."* *⁹"Then, Lord," Simon Peter replied, "not just my feet but my hands and my head as well!" ¹⁰Jesus answered, "Those who have had a bath need only to wash their feet; their whole body is clean. And you are clean, though not every one of you." . . .*

Understanding the Word. Once again in this narrative we have a word used in two very different ways: a mundane sense and a spiritual sense. The word in this case is "clean." The story begins with Peter being nonplussed that Jesus would even think of washing his feet, hence his question. As he so often does, Jesus does not respond directly but rather obliquely—"You do not realize now what I am doing, but later you will understand." This assumes that there will be a later, a time when Peter will reflect back on events like this during the ministry and grasp their significance. Notice however that Jesus does not say, "Unless you understand and embrace what's happening now, you shouldn't participate in this." Unfortunately, some people take this approach to sacraments like baptism or the Lord's Supper, which is a mistake. Sacraments are outward and visible signs of God's grace, not of our human response to God's grace, as is also the case with this act of foot washing, and as such it should just be received. The understanding can come later suggests Jesus.

Peter then objects strongly to what Jesus is about to do, saying, "You shall never wash my feet." Apparently Peter thought Jesus had crossed the line from humility to humiliation of himself. He wasn't a household servant or slave!

Jesus' rebuttal is "Unless I wash you, you have no part in me." This suggests that this symbolic ritual is meant to signify the internal cleansing of a person—his heart, his mind, his emotions, and his will. Typical of Peter, now his reaction is to totally flip-flop. He goes from saying, "You will never, ever wash my feet" to "Shoot, let's not stop with the feet; wash everything!"

This must have produced something of a wry smile from Jesus, and so he adds, "Well, actually, you've already had the bath, so all you need now is the periodic cleansing of the feet." When Jesus affirms they are clean, he is referring to the spiritual transformation of the disciples, except, of course, Judas, who is just the opposite—spiritually dirty.

This portion of the narrative concludes with the editorial comment (of which there are many in this gospel, again reminding us that the audience must have needed such commentary, suggesting a neophyte audience) that Jesus said what he did because he knew who would betray him. It is a remarkable act of love to continue to love and serve someone you know is going to betray you. But that is just what happens in this episode. Jesus must surely have washed Judas's feet as well as the others.

1. What do you think of the act of foot washing as a Christian practice?

2. What do you make of Jesus' choice of actions when he knew his time was running out?

3. While most people might well choose to focus on spending time with their immediate families in the shadow of death, Jesus spends time with his disciples. What do you make of this choice?

THREE

The Imitation of Christ

John 13:12–21 *When he had finished washing their feet, he put on his clothes and returned to his place. "Do you understand what I have done for you?" he asked them. ¹³"You call me 'Teacher' and 'Lord,' and rightly so, for that is what I am. ¹⁴Now that I, your Lord and Teacher, have washed your feet, you also should wash one another's feet. ¹⁵I have set you an example that you should do as I have done for you. ¹⁶Very truly I tell you, no servant is greater than his master, nor is a messenger greater than the one who sent him. ¹⁷Now that you know these things, you will be blessed if you do them. ¹⁸I am not referring to all of you; I know those I have chosen. But this is to fulfill this passage of Scripture: 'He who shared my bread has turned against me.' ¹⁹I am telling you now before it happens, so that when it does happen you will believe that I am who I am. ²⁰Very truly I tell you, whoever accepts anyone I send accepts me; and whoever accepts me accepts the one who sent me." ²¹After he had said this, Jesus was troubled in spirit and testified, "Very truly I tell you, one of you is going to betray me."*

Understanding the Word. It is interesting, perhaps a strange irony of this gospel, that while it neither mandates baptism nor the Lord's Supper as a Christian practice, Jesus does say that the disciples should follow his lead and wash each other's feet. He even says there will be blessing if this imperative is followed. Perhaps the majority of the church has been missing out on a blessing for centuries now.

In ancient pedagogy, one of the major features of teaching was modeling. The students were taught to imitate their teachers. This was not a power move; it was a principle move. Just as Jesus has modeled the behavior of a servant, so the disciples should follow his lead and do the same. Jesus sets the example, and in the same breath affirms what they all know—that they are right to say he is their master and teacher. There are many ways in which we cannot imitate Christ (for example, dying on a cross to save the world or inaugurating a new covenant), but there are many ways we can, and we are urged here to do so.

In view of the word "clean" being a double entendre in this passage, it may be worth asking what the function of this ritual might be if practiced by Christians on each other. One obvious answer is that this is a humbling thing to do, both for the foot washer and for the recipient. It builds a servant attitude and approach to working together as Christ's followers. One also wondered if it might not be connected to something Jesus' brother advised: "Confess your sins to each other" (James 5:16). Confession is indeed a means of internal cleansing and can lead to forgiveness, something Jesus tells his disciples they are all empowered to offer others after the Resurrection (John 20:23).

Psalm 41:9 is cited in this context, and it is important to note that the Passion narratives are loaded with quotes, allusions, and echoes to Old Testament passages, and with good reason. This was the part of the story most difficult to explain and justify to a world that was not looking for a servant leader, much less a crucified messiah. For a world who wanted a leader that said, "Let's get ready to rumble," they got a leader that said, "Let's get ready to serve and love, even to the point of dying a slave's death on a cross, if need be." Later in this gospel, in John 21, Jesus will tell Peter that he is heading to the same end as he came to in Golgotha.

Jesus talks about "knowing those whom I have chosen." This seems to refer to something more than just the call to discipleship, because clearly even Judas was called to be a follower by Jesus. The question that is not answered here is: Chosen for what? The context however strongly suggests that what is meant is chosen for service of Christ and one another. Nothing is said here about everlasting salvation being a result of being chosen.

Lest the disciples get too big for their britches, Jesus reminds them that a servant is not greater than their master, or a sent one greater than the one doing the sending. If it was enough for Jesus to act self-sacrificially, there is no reason for the disciples to think this was beneath their dignity or not their calling!

Verse 19 suggests there is a good reason why Jesus is telling the disciples this, including predicting his own betrayal. When the prophecy comes true, says Jesus, then you will have confirmation that "I am" (see the comments earlier in this study regarding *ego eimi*). This may suggest that the confirmation makes clear that Jesus is "the Great I Am." At minimum it means that Jesus had told them the truth in advance, and so at minimum he was a true prophet.

The end of this segment makes clear how very deeply it upset Jesus that one of the disciples was going to betray him. After all, he had spent three long years with them, and yet, in the end, Jesus could see that it was going to end badly in some cases. If Jesus had not loved his disciples, he might not have had this reaction, but he did. He even loved Judas to the end.

1. This passage suggests that some things should be taken by faith, trusting one will understand them later. How do you feel about that?

2. What do you think about the idea of teachers modeling the behavior their students should emulate, rather than just teaching them a subject matter?

3. How does this passage depict humility?

FOUR

"Lord, Is It I?"

John 13:22–30 *His disciples stared at one another, at a loss to know which of them he meant. ²³One of them, the disciple whom Jesus loved, was reclining* *next to him. ²⁴Simon Peter motioned to this disciple and said, "Ask him which one he means." ²⁵Leaning back against Jesus, he asked him, "Lord, who is it?" ²⁶Jesus answered, "It is the one to whom I will give this piece of bread when I have dipped it in the dish." Then, dipping the piece of bread, he gave it to Judas, the son of Simon Iscariot. ²⁷As soon as Judas took the bread, Satan entered into him. So Jesus told him, "What you are about to do, do quickly." ²⁸But no one at the meal understood why Jesus said this to him. ²⁹Since Judas had charge of the money, some thought Jesus was telling him to buy what was needed for the festival, or to give something to the poor. ³⁰As soon as Judas had taken the bread, he went out. And it was night.*

Understanding the Word. The disciples are shocked by Jesus' prediction of his betrayal. Clearly they had not looked deep inside themselves to realize that any one of them could have been the man. The proof of this is not long in coming, as Jesus will go on to indicate that the leader of the Twelve is going to deny knowing Jesus not once, not twice, but three times in a very short span of time, and all just to save his own neck. This is not the servant leadership and example Jesus was setting and talking about.

Notice Peter motions to the Beloved Disciple and asks him to ask Jesus who will be the betrayer, because the Beloved Disciple is reclining on the same couch with Jesus. Jesus answers, but indirectly, saying, "It is the one to whom I give this piece of bread when I have dipped it in the dish." This should be compared to the Markan account, where Jesus says, "It is one of the Twelve . . . one who dips bread into the bowl with me" (Mark 14:20). The gist of these two versions of the saying is the same, but it is instructive to notice the differences, as it reminds us that both accounts as we have them are now in Greek, and neither one of them is likely to be an exact translation of the Aramaic. The gospel writers had a certain freedom under inspiration to translate and paraphrase and arrange materials according to their overarching purposes. The Gospels are not digital pictures of these events. They are interpretive portraits, with each Evangelist adding something to the overall understanding of the Christ event.

If previously we heard that Satan was prompting Judas's behavior, now at verse 27 we hear something worse, something like demon possession. It says "Satan entered him" at this juncture, just as soon as he took the bread.

Jesus then says, "What you are about to do, do quickly," and Judas goes out from the meal. The Evangelist, punctuating the very character of what was happening, says dramatically at the end of this segment, "and it was night." The time of true darkness in Jesus' story had arrived. We are told quite clearly that none of the disciples present, not even Peter or the Beloved Disciple, understood what Judas was doing. The guess was that since he was the treasurer, he was going out to make preparations for the festival.

On a historical front, this conjecture is important, as it probably makes clear that the meal with the foot washing took place early in the week, and so it was assumed that Judas went out to make preparations for Passover by buying the lamb, and so forth. Our Evangelist has left the traces of that early meal right in front of us at the beginning and end of the story. But in the middle he has intercalated a bit from the Last Supper, as if he told that story as well. It would be three meals in a row (John 12, 13, 14), but what he wants to do next is group together the after-dinner teachings of Jesus given during several nights during that week in John 13:21–17. It sufficed to present one combo presentation of the meals of Passover Week, and one combo presentation of the various teachings done during the week.

1. Why were meals such important events in the life of Jesus, especially during the last week of his ministry?

2. What do you think Jesus meant by saying the disciples were clean?

3. Was Jesus actually encouraging Judas to get on with betraying him when he said, "What you are about to do, do quickly"?

FIVE

Simon Says

John 13:31–38 *When he was gone, Jesus said, "Now the Son of Man is glorified and God is glorified in him. ³²If God is glorified in him, God will glorify the Son in himself, and will glorify him at once. ³³My children, I will be with you only a little longer. You will look for me, and just as I told the Jews, so I tell you now: Where I am going, you cannot come. ³⁴A new command I give* *you: Love one another. As I have loved you, so you must love one another.* ³⁵*By this everyone will know that you are my disciples, if you love one another."* ³⁶*Simon Peter asked him, "Lord, where are you going?" Jesus replied, "Where I am going, you cannot follow now, but you will follow later." * ³⁷*Peter asked, "Lord, why can't I follow you now? I will lay down my life for you." * ³⁸*Then Jesus answered, "Will you really lay down your life for me? Very truly I tell you, before the rooster crows, you will disown me three times!"*

Understanding the Word. The Farewell Discourse actually begins here, in the context of this meal, and immediately the first words out of Jesus' mouth raise a question: In what way is the Son of Man glorified by his betrayal and what ensues from it? Furthermore, how is God the Father glorified by, in, and through what comes next?

In verse 33, Jesus tenderly calls his disciples "my children" (*teknia*). It's as if he is going back to square one, and feels he has to instruct them all over again. And in particular he has to stress he's leaving, and soon! He reminds them of what he told the Jewish officials, namely, where he is going now, they cannot follow at present. They will look for him in vain. Here is the point at which he chooses to give his disciples a new commandment— "Love one another. As I have loved you, so you must love one another." This is not optional. It is something Jesus insists they must do. But how? Loving one another in the way, to the degree, and with the grace and depth of the love that Jesus showed them. How could they ever manage that? The commandment is ironic in this context where Jesus has just talked about being betrayed by one member of his inner circle, and he is about to refer to his being denied by another, the very leader of the Twelve. It is much like when Augustine said, "You must give what you command, Lord, and then command whatsoever you will." It would be totally impossible if God's love were not poured into human hearts. It is interesting that the term *Maundy Thursday* comes from the Latin word *Mandatum*, or mandate. The mandate that was given on that Thursday was to love one another as Christ loved us. The term was garbled into *Maundy* in Old English. Jesus is saying that when all else fails, if you want to know what is most important, it is this.

It is Peter, the Twelve's spokesman, who asks, "And where precisely are you going, Jesus?" Irony is piled upon irony as this dialogue progresses. Jesus replies that where he is going, Peter cannot follow him now, but will do so later. Peter protests (and here comes the irony), "I will lay down my life for you." But of course it was going to be just the other way around. What Peter was going to do was put the whole discipling process into reverse!

"Will you really lay down your life for me?" asks Jesus. "In fact, not so much," says Jesus. "Instead, before this very night is out, before the cock crows [the name of the last watch of the night] you will disown me three separate times!" If truth in a Jewish court was confirmed by a twofold testimony, then threefold denial cannot be good! At the very least it is an emphatic denial. This pronouncement must have shocked everyone in the room. Everyone. I can hear Bob Dylan singing in the background here: "It's not dark yet, but it's getting there."

1. Why do you think Jesus called his disciples "little children" here?

2. What do you make of Peter's protest that he was ready to lay down his life for Jesus? Was this mere bravado? Or do you think he was sincere, but wilted under pressure?

3. Does Jesus give a clue to Peter about his future when he says he will one day follow Jesus where he is going? Is it a ray of hope beyond denials, or just a prediction of martyrdom, or some of both?

COMMENTARY NOTES

General Comments. Throughout this gospel we have agency language—language about people being sent, and about the One who sent them. The Father sends the Son, the Son sends the Spirit, the Son and the Spirit send the disciples. Agency language in early Judaism had a very specific sense and valence. The Hebrew verb was *shalach* (send), which is probably the origin of the term *apostolos*, which literally means "someone sent out for some purpose." For example, there was a saying in Jesus' day: "A man's agent is as himself." What was meant by this is that when a master sent his agent out to do business for him, the agent was to be treated by the recipient as if he were the one who had sent him. He was to be given the same respect, the same food, the same hospitality, because the agent had been empowered and had the same authority as the sender, at least in the matters for which he had been authorized. So it was between Jesus and his disciples.

The paradox has been often observed that this gospel, more than any other, emphasizes Jesus is the apostle, the "sent one" of the Father, and equally that the Spirit is the "sent one" of the Son. The language of agency is used repeatedly in the same gospel that tells us that Jesus is God the Son, just as the Spirit is God the Spirit, the living presence of God on the earth. Agency language is about authorization, empowerment, mission, relationship, and function, not necessarily about nature or ontology. The God language tells us who Jesus is, the agency language tells us who sent him and what his relationship is to the sender. Hence, no disciple could ever become bigger or greater than his master. He would always have derived authority and empowerment, not inherent theology and empowerment.

Day 3. The two portions of Scripture most frequently used in messianic ways to explain Jesus and the story of Jesus are the Psalms and Isaiah 40–66. There are literally hundreds of quotes, allusions, or echoes to these sources of material. The Psalms, of course, were originally songs, sung in Hebrew worship. They were not *inherently* prophecies. Isaiah is a different matter. It definitely was prophecy. Care needs to be taken in figuring out *how* the Old Testament is used in the New Testament. It is truly a complex matter. It is one thing to say that a text was inherently messianic or about the messiah in the intention of the original human author. It is another thing to talk about the appropriate messianic use of some non-messianic material. But even this way of putting it is not the whole story, for if indeed the Old Testament is part of God's inspired Word, then it can be argued that certainly God knew in advance these texts would be used by Jesus and his followers. It does seem clear enough that Jesus was one of the major instigators of the practice of his followers reading the Old Testament in light of the Christ event. This is exactly what texts like Mark 12:35–37 suggest, or Luke 24:27, 46. Jesus taught the disciples to read the Scriptures in this way. What this really suggests is not that the Old Testament literally predicted everything about Jesus, even in the non-prophetic portions of it, but rather that Jesus was, as Paul would say, "the yea and Amen." He was the fulfillment or fulfiller of all the promises and prophecies of the Old Testament. Thus, in the Gospel of John, Jesus is even seen as the fulfillment of Jewish institutions (which are not in themselves prophecies), such as the Sabbath, the Passover sacrifice, the Temple, and so on. Prediction is one thing; fulfillment is another. In short, it is one thing to say the whole Old Testament in some sense points to Jesus, and he fulfills it all, including its Law. It is another thing to say that the Old Testament predicts the whole gospel story and everything about Jesus.

It is a mistake to try to find Jesus under every rock in the Old Testament. There was no incarnation before the incarnation spoken of in John 1. For example, Jesus was not the angel of the Lord who wrestled with Jacob, or one of the mysterious visitors to Abraham's tent. The New Testament does not make claims like that. Indeed the book of Hebrews urges us to read the Old Testament typologically, not reading Jesus back into Old Testament events here, there, and yonder. Melchizedek is a type of Christ, but he is not a previous visit of Jesus to earth. The Old Testament foreshadows what is to come, prepares for what is to come, predicts to some degree what is to come, but it is not a total guide or road map for what eventually transpired.

One must have a sense of progressive revelation and allow the Old Testament to be the before and the New Testament to be the after of God's revelation. Otherwise, the whole history of Israel just becomes a cipher for Christ and the church. But Jesus was one greater than Moses, greater than David, greater than Isaiah, greater even than the angel of the Lord. These were only prefigures and preparations for the gospel. History and its development matters even in terms of salvation, and so a flat reading of the whole Bible—or a total Christianizing of the Old Testament—will not do because it disrespects the history, and the difference between the previous prophets, priests, and kings, and Jesus on the one hand, and the difference between Israel and the church on the other.

WEEK EIGHT

GATHERING DISCUSSION OUTLINE

A. Open session in prayer.

B. View video for this week's readings.

C. What general impressions and thoughts do you have after considering the video, readings, and the daily writings on these Scriptures?

D. Discuss questions based on the daily readings.

1. **KEY OBSERVATION:** No matter how many times one reads the story of Passion Week, there is surely something in all of us that has at least a little hope. Maybe this time things will turn out better. Sometimes it really is necessary for things to get pitch black before there can be a dawn.

   DISCUSSION QUESTION: Have you ever had that thought in reading the Passion narratives? Why do you think Jesus had to go through betrayal, denial, desertion, and death en route to his resurrection?

2. **KEY OBSERVATION:** Sometimes the Twelve look more like the Dirty Dozen than the Terrific Twelve. And of course we can relate to this. Sometimes we are not as faithful as we should be, not as truthful as we should be, wilt under pressure, or run away when the going gets tough.

   DISCUSSION QUESTION: In what ways can you relate to the Twelve?

3. **KEY OBSERVATION:** It is noticeable that here at the end, Jesus takes great pains to instruct his disciples at length, realizing they would not

understand much of what he said until after the fact, and in some cases, long after the fact.

DISCUSSION QUESTION: Have you ever been the teacher who waits patiently for your students to get it? What lesson can we learn from Jesus' example?

4. **KEY OBSERVATION:** It was Socrates who said, "Know thyself," but few people really do. One may think he knows how he would respond to a crisis, until he gets there and discovers that he responded very differently, and in a less flattering way than he had aspired to.

   DISCUSSION QUESTION: Do you think Peter was sincere in his saying that he would lay down his life for Jesus?

5. **KEY OBSERVATION:** Life lived unto God is teleological—it has a purpose and a goal. Each person should search out his or her calling and pursue it. A big part of Jesus' calling was to love his disciples to the end.

   DISCUSSION QUESTION: What would the church look like if we actually lived into this calling?

E. What facts and information presented in the commentary portion of the lesson help you understand the weekly Scripture?

F. Close session with prayer.

WEEK NINE

John 15:1–16:15

Farewell Discourse

INTRODUCTION

We are well and truly in the middle of the Farewell Discourse in John 15–16. Notice how at the end of John 14 we have a conclusion to one discourse, with Jesus saying, "Come. Let's leave." There is a lot of repetition in these discourses of the same terms, the same themes, and the same exhortations, so it really isn't necessary to go through it all in a study like this. You will get the thrust of it in what we are about to discuss, and we need to notice from the outset that it involves both theology and ethics, both indicatives and imperatives. It is not just one long, final harangue saying, "Do this; do that." We will focus, then, on one important representative sampling in the middle of these teachings.

ONE

The Genuine Divine Vine

John 15:1–8 *"I am the true vine, and my Father is the gardener. ²He cuts off every branch in me that bears no fruit, while every branch that does bear fruit he prunes so that it will be even more fruitful. ³You are already clean because of the word I have spoken to you. Remain in me, as I also remain in you. ⁴No branch can bear fruit by itself; it must remain in the vine. Neither can you bear fruit unless you remain in me. ⁵I am the vine; you are the branches. If you remain in me and I in you, you will bear much fruit; apart from me you can do nothing. ⁶If you do not remain in me, you are like a branch that is thrown away and withers; such branches are picked up, thrown into the fire* *and burned. ⁷If you remain in me and my words remain in you, ask whatever you wish, and it will be done for you. ⁸This is to my Father's glory, that you bear much fruit, showing yourselves to be my disciples."*

Understanding the Word. Vines and olive trees became symbols for the people of God, things that God could grow or prune, things from which God expected fruit. Jesus begins his discussion here by saying that he himself is the vine, and God the gardener. He suggests that the disciples are like branches off of the central vine. What he in fact calls himself is the "genuine (or authentic) vine." "True" here has the sense of authentic as opposed to phony, not true as opposed to false. This suggests that there are other vines out there, but Jesus' disciples should not accept substitutes. One of the things scholars say about a passage like this is that it suggests that Jesus sees himself as an incorporative personality; that is, others can be grafted into or joined to him. It is the kind of thing Paul is talking about when he says believers are "in Christ." In fact he never uses the term *Christian.* He always says we are in Christ. Obviously there are Old Testament precedents for this sort of language. For example, the people of Israel are called God's vineyard in Isaiah 5:1–7. But here it is one person, Jesus himself, who is said to be the vine.

We are told from the outset that God, the gardener, prunes this vine, lopping off unproductive branches and pruning those that are productive. Without wishing to press the imagery too hard, the mention of lopping off seems to make clear that one could genuinely be in the vine, and then later out of it, due to non-productivity. In other words, apostasy is possible even for those genuinely in the vine at some juncture. But all the branches should expect pruning along the way so that they might be more fruitful. Pruning of the sort mentioned can be painful, but in the long run productive.

A little knowledge of horticulture comes in handy here. Branches do not produce fruit by being sapsuckers, sucking the nutrition out of the vine. To the contrary, the vine pushes its vital substances into the branches so they will be productive. In other words, it's not all on the branches to be productive. Biblical scholar F. F. Bruce once said, "Trees do not produce fruit by acts of Parliament," by which he meant that mere laws or exhortations also do not get the job done. It takes a close connection between the vine and the branches.

We hear a bit more about being clean at this juncture (see John 13), and are told that God's Word is the cleansing agent. This leads to a moment's meditation: What is the condition of a church that is biblically illiterate? Answer: No wonder we have so many problems and sins cropping up in the church.

Jesus does indeed give an exhortation to the branches. It's not all about sitting around and expecting God to make something of your life. Jesus says to "keep on abiding" or "remaining in me." This implies ongoing effort. The verb tense is present, continual. In other words, we must make the effort to abide in Christ, whatever that may entail, and it's the key to being fruitful in our Christian lives.

But then at verse 5 we have a promise: "If you remain in me and I in you, you *will* bear much fruit." *However*—and it is a big however—if you don't, you will not accomplish a darn thing. There follows a warning that fire is in your future if you don't abide and don't bear fruit.

It is crucial not to take verse 7 out of context. It doesn't say, "Ask whatever you will in my name and you will receive it," despite the prosperity preachers on TV. There is a condition to this promise: "If you remain in me, and my words remain in you, ask whatever you wish." What this means, of course, is that if you are well-grounded in the Word, you are not about to ask for something that contradicts the teaching of Jesus! You're not going to pray (as Janis Joplin sang), "Oh, Lord, won't you buy me a Mercedes Benz." Why not? *Because that is not the way Jesus lived*, and we are supposed to be following his example, not justifying our own conspicuous consumption by misquoting Bible verses! Jesus lived a life of self-sacrifice, not a life of self-indulgence. Furthermore, elsewhere in this gospel Jesus talks about asking "in my name." But here's the point. If you are going to sign Jesus' name to a prayer, you better have lined it up first by asking: Is this something Jesus himself would have prayed for? If not, don't pray it.

Finally, Jesus says that we demonstrate we are Jesus' disciples by bearing much fruit. So how's your crop been coming along?

1. Why is abiding important, and what role do you have in making sure that happens?

2. What in your life needs some pruning so you can bear more fruit?

3. What sort of things do you think Jesus encourages us to ask for from God?

TWO

The Love Command

John 15:9–17 *"As the Father has loved me, so have I loved you. Now remain in my love. ¹⁰If you keep my commands, you will remain in my love, just as I have kept my Father's commands and remain in his love. ¹¹I have told you this so that my joy may be in you and that your joy may be complete. ¹²My command is this: Love each other as I have loved you. ¹³Greater love has no one than this: to lay down one's life for one's friends. ¹⁴You are my friends if you do what I command. ¹⁵I no longer call you servants, because a servant does not know his master's business. Instead, I have called you friends, for everything that I learned from my Father I have made known to you. ¹⁶You did not choose me, but I chose you and appointed you so that you might go and bear fruit—fruit that will last—and so that whatever you ask in my name the Father will give you. ¹⁷This is my command: Love each other."*

Understanding the Word. In this section, which is a natural development of the previous one, Jesus is still talking about abiding or remaining, but in this case it is about abiding in Jesus' love. Here we are given some clue as to how to go about that—"If you keep my commands, you will remain in my love"—but the main command is to love one another. Sometimes Christians are guilty of thinking that their relationship with the Lord is private. When other things go awry in life, there's still their relationship with the Lord. But, in fact, this passage suggests a different view. It suggests that we should be focusing on loving each other, and by that very process we will abide in Christ's love. Instead of navel gazing or focusing too intently on your personal walk with the Lord, Jesus is suggesting more focus on your neighbor, your friends, your fellow disciples, and then your relationship with the Lord will be fine.

Jesus tells us that he has loved us in the same way the Father has loved him—lavishly, abundantly, continually. But this does not mean that the Father would not ask difficult things of the Son. Indeed, he asked him to come and die for a largely ungrateful, unprepared, unreceptive group of creatures—human beings. Sometimes Christians think and even say things like: "God would never ask me to do that!" For example, they say, "God would never ask me to lay down my life for my friends. After all, I have a family to think of, a good job, and a wife who wants me around." While these are natural thoughts, they are not always godly thoughts. Sometimes God really does want us to lay down our lives for others, to make big sacrifices for someone other than our immediate family. It is interesting that in all this talk of love in John 13–17, not once does Jesus exhort us to love our physical families. Maybe he simply assumed that would happen, but it is also true that he thought the family of faith was the primary family, and the physical family one's secondary family, especially if the latter was not a part of the former. This is exactly what Jesus says in Mark 3:31–35, though we still have a difficult time living into the idea.

Jesus adds another incentive for keeping this commandment—namely, we evolve from just servant of the King to being a friend of the King. Jesus will friend you if you behave in this manner! With being Jesus' friend comes inside information. Jesus says we will be in the know about the Father's business, will have an understanding of what bearing fruit, doing ministry, and loving others is really all about.

We are also reminded that we were not chosen by Jesus just to be saved people. Salvation is just a means to the real end, which is that we might bear fruit, love God and others better, and in fact produce fruit that really lasts, fruit that doesn't spoil or disappear quickly, fruit that doesn't have a best-by date on it. It is when you bear lasting fruit, realizing you've been saved to serve others, that you are then on the right track. You've gotten out of your self-centered ways, and then are in a position to ask God for anything that is in accord with the Father's will, anything that you could sign God's name to.

1. Why do you think there is so much stress on love and on commanding love in the New Testament? Has Jesus raised the bar impossibly high?

2. How does one get to be a friend of Jesus?

3. In this passage, what is said to be the greatest love we could show?

THREE

Hate Crimes

John 15:18–25 *"If the world hates you, keep in mind that it hated me first. ¹⁹If you belonged to the world, it would love you as its own. As it is, you do not belong to the world, but I have chosen you out of the world. That is why the world hates you. ²⁰Remember what I told you: 'A servant is not greater than his master.' If they persecuted me, they will persecute you also. If they obeyed my teaching, they will obey yours also. ²¹They will treat you this way because of my name, for they do not know the one who sent me. ²²If I had not come and spoken to them, they would not be guilty of sin; but now they have no excuse for their sin. ²³Whoever hates me hates my Father as well. ²⁴If I had not done among them the works no one else did, they would not be guilty of sin. As it is, they have seen, and yet they have hated both me and my Father. ²⁵But this is to fulfill what is written in their Law: 'They hated me without reason.'"*

Understanding the Word. *Hate* is a very strong word. We hear a lot of talk about hate speech, hate crimes, or even phrases like "don't be a hater." Hate is often just pure emotion, not rational at all, so it is not entirely a surprise that Jesus says that he was hated without reason, in fact alluding to a couple of passages in the Psalms (35:19; 69:4). In the truth in advertising department, Jesus is warning his disciples that they are likely to be despised, persecuted, prosecuted, and even executed just as he was. A servant should not expect any better treatment than the Master received. Jesus says that they didn't really know him; they didn't know the one who sent him—God the Father.

With knowledge comes responsibility. Jesus says that when he came and shared his Word, the listeners became responsible for how they responded. He adds that if he had not come and done the mighty works he did, they would not be responsible or guilty for rejecting him. This is an interesting point. If Jesus had come and simply lived a normal life, worked as a carpenter, supported his family and the like, and not done what God sent him to earth to do, then their reaction to Jesus would not have incurred considerable guilt. It is precisely because they did hear the truth that they became responsible for what they did with what they heard, especially if they despised it and treated the speaker with hatred.

There is a strong contrast in this passage between the world and the circle of disciples. It is because the disciples don't belong to the world, don't emulate the ways of the world, don't bow down to the gods of this world, and so on, that they are ridiculed, rejected, and even hated. Christians then and Christians now have been accused of being spoilsports and killjoys because they will not play ball with the sinful ways of the world, and so they stand out as an easy target for abuse. It is true to say that the less and less a culture is Christian in character, the more and more Christians will stand out like a sore thumb. And so Jesus warns about the coming criticism, condemnation, and worse. Perhaps worst of all, a person who hates Jesus actually hates God the Father as well. Some think they can ignore Jesus and still love God, or worse, think they can reject Jesus, and still love God. But this forgets that God is above all the Father of Jesus, and he who has seen Jesus has seen the Father. It's a sort of package deal—if you reject the Son, you've also rejected the Father, and as Jesus adds, if they reject his disciples, they should know this implies a rejection of God as well.

1. Why do you think a person as loving as Jesus suffered from so much rejection and even hatred?

2. One of the themes of this gospel is that knowledge implies moral responsibility. Paul suggests the same sort of thing when he says that where there is no law, there is no willful violation of that law. What sort of moral responsibility do you think Christians have to share the gospel?

3. Jesus says he has chosen his disciples out of this world. What do you think that means?

FOUR

The Advocate

John 15:26–16:11 *"When the Advocate comes, whom I will send to you from the Father—the Spirit of truth who goes out from the Father—he will* *testify about me. ²⁷And you also must testify, for you have been with me from the beginning. ¹All this I have told you so that you will not fall away. ²They will put you out of the synagogue; in fact, the time is coming when anyone who kills you will think they are offering a service to God. ³They will do such things because they have not known the Father or me. ⁴I have told you this, so that when their time comes you will remember that I warned you about them. I did not tell you this from the beginning because I was with you, ⁵but now I am going to him who sent me. None of you asks me, 'Where are you going?' ⁶Rather, you are filled with grief because I have said these things. ⁷But very truly I tell you, it is for your good that I am going away. Unless I go away, the Advocate will not come to you; but if I go, I will send him to you. ⁸When he comes, he will prove the world to be in the wrong about sin and righteousness and judgment: ⁹about sin, because people do not believe in me; ¹⁰about righteousness, because I am going to the Father, where you can see me no longer; ¹¹and about judgment, because the prince of this world now stands condemned."*

Understanding the Word. The Greek term *parakletos* has sometimes been mistranslated as "comforter." This has led to all sorts of maudlin images of the Holy Spirit and his role in our lives. In fact, the term has a forensic sense, meaning a counselor or legal advocate, which is how the word is being used in the Scripture above. In the Farewell Discourses, Jesus indicates that the Holy Spirit is another *parakletos,* implying that he was the first one. He was the Advocate sent by the Father, and the Spirit is the Advocate sent by the Son when he goes back to heaven. It is this role of Advocate that explains the emphasis on his roles of convicting the world of sin, convincing the believer, and persuading one or another person about the truth. In a sense, the Spirit is the lawyer for the defense of Jesus. Of course the analogy should not be over-pressed, as the Spirit has other, nonlegal roles as well, for instance, sanctifying the believer. Nonetheless, we hear that the Advocate will prove the world wrong about sin, righteousness, and judgment (v. 8). This is all within the normal purview and job description of a legal advocate.

Jesus told his disciples what he did so that they would not fall away. There would be no need to say this to the disciples if falling away from the truth was impossible. No one likes to be rejected. Indeed, most people would like to be loved, but Jesus warns against basing one's actions on being popular or pleasing. Rather, their job is to be faithful to the truth, thereby pleasing God, and if the audience responds negatively, Jesus had warned the disciples about it. The worst would be like Paul when he was Saul—he thought he was pleasing and serving God by persecuting Christians. Being ejected from the synagogue was based on the rejecter's ignorance of God and Jesus. Forewarned is forearmed, apparently, and so Jesus says he reserved this bad news until now because he is leaving. While he was with them, he could take the brunt of the criticism directly.

Jesus also suggests his going away is a sort of good news/bad news situation. On the one hand it will cause the disciples to grieve. On the other hand, it is necessary that he go, so he can send the Spirit to them. It has been suggested, in view of the focus of the Old Testament on the Father, that apparently humankind can only deal with one member of the Trinity on earth at a time—first the Father, then the Son, then the Spirit. A moment's reflection however will show this is a caricature, since we hear about all three working in the world in the book of Acts after Pentecost.

The good news at the end of this passage is that the prince of this world stands condemned. The work of Christ was not just about overcoming human sin. It was also about dealing with supernatural evil. We have already heard about the devil in John as someone who goaded and then entered into Judas, prompting the betrayal of Jesus. He is the manipulator of evil behind the scenes. Lest we think it was always about human misdeeds, we are reminded by Paul that our battle is not mainly against flesh and blood, but against principalities and powers. This is important to keep in mind, lest we demonize other human beings who disagree with or even despise us. God has a plan for the future of the prince of darkness, and so the disciples need not worry about that sort of thing.

1. What is your understanding of the Holy Spirit? Is the Spirit a person?

2. Jesus says that a good deal of what he has been saying is to prevent the disciples from falling away. What do you think about Christians and apostasy?

3. If someone rejects Jesus out of sheer ignorance, is he or she guilty of sin according to Jesus?

FIVE

Unbearable Truths

John 16:12–15 *"I have much more to say to you, more than you can now bear. [13]But when he, the Spirit of truth, comes, he will guide you into all the truth. He will not speak on his own; he will speak only what he hears, and he will tell you what is yet to come. [14]He will glorify me because it is from me that he will receive what he will make known to you. [15]All that belongs to the Father is mine. That is why I said the Spirit will receive from me what he will make known to you."*

Understanding the Word. The disciples are told that Jesus has much more to say to them, but he figures they are on information overload already. However, when the Spirit comes, he will lead the disciples into all the truth they need to know. As the Advocate of the Son, he will not be offering new truths that originated with the Spirit; rather, he will speak what he hears from Jesus and about the future. The Spirit is going to glorify the Son, and we are told the reason why: "It is from me that he will receive what he will make known to you." There is an interesting rationale given as to why the Spirit will operate the way he does—"all that belongs to the Father is mine." That is, the Spirit is not the originator of new truths; the Spirit glorifies the Son because the Son is sharing with the Spirit what his Father has given Jesus—namely, everything. This leads to the quite proper conclusion that the Holy Spirit does not and would not say anything that does not build on or comport with the words of Jesus that he spoke while on earth. Whatever new words from the Lord may come to the disciples post-Easter, they will not be truly new, novel, weird, or strange, much less contradictory to the teaching of Jesus. That's just not how the Spirit works as the Advocate and speaker for Jesus.

It is perhaps worth adding that when Jesus says "truth," he is talking about Truth, not trivial things like "there are clouds in the sky," or "grass is green," and so on. In particular, we are talking about salvific truth, truth about the human condition, truth about God, truth about Christ, truth about sin, and so on. It is right, then, to realize that we do not expect the Holy Spirit to teach us on just any and all subjects. Then too, when we hear people saying things like, "The Spirit told me to tell you that I don't need to take classes to fully understand the Bible; I can just read it," you can be sure this message did not come from the Holy Spirit. The Holy Spirit is not anti-education, nor is the Spirit pro-ignorance. Ignorance is not bliss, when it comes to truth, including God's truth.

1. What is the role of the Holy Spirit in your life?

2. It has been said that the Spirit convicts, convinces, and converts, and is also a guide into all the truth that one needs to be saved and lead a godly life. What have you learned from listening to the Spirit speaking into your life?

3. What personal traits does this material attribute to the Holy Spirit?

COMMENTARY NOTES

General Comments. There are five Paraclete (Holy Spirit) sayings (see Day Four) in the Fourth Gospel, and every single one of them is found in the four Farewell Discourses (14:26; 15:26; 16:7–11, 12–15). This is not a surprise since this entire final teaching section was intended to prepare and equip the disciples for their roles as Christian witnesses once Jesus was gone, and so it was directed specifically to them, not to the general public.

The fact that both Jesus and the Spirit are called *parakletos* suggests strongly that the Son and the Spirit should be seen as having the same agenda, sharing the same truth, and even having the same functions when it comes to the truth. The language of agency lurks in the background as well (see the discussion earlier in this study), and not surprisingly the same sort of language is applied to the disciples themselves in 15:18–27. Here we can note that among the other roles of the Spirit not mentioned thus far are: he is to indwell the disciples, conveying the presence, power, and peace of God (see 14:17–27); he is to testify to the believer about Jesus (14:26; 15:26); and he is to enable the disciples to testify to the world effectively so that like the Spirit and by means of the Spirit they convict, convince, and convert the world.

The teaching about the Holy Spirit seems to reflect some knowledge of some things said in the Wisdom of Solomon (found in the Apocryphal books) about the Spirit. For example consider the Wisdom of Solomon 1:4–9:

> Wisdom will not enter a deceitful soul, or dwell in a body enslaved to sin. ⁵For a holy and disciplined spirit will flee from deceit, and will leave foolish thoughts behind, and will be ashamed at the approach of unrighteousness. ⁶For wisdom is a kindly spirit, but will not free blasphemers from the guilt of their words; because God is witness of their inmost feelings, and a true observer of their hearts, and hearer of their tongues. ⁷Because the Spirit of the Lord has filled the world, and that which holds all things together knows what is said; ⁸therefore those who utter unrighteous things will not escape notice, and justice, when it punishes, will not pass them by. ⁹For inquiry will be made into the counsels of the ungodly, and a report of their words will come to the Lord, to convict them of their lawless deeds. (NRSVACE)

Or consider Wisdom of Solomon 9:17–18:

> "Who has learned your counsel, unless you have given wisdom and sent your holy spirit from on high?

¹⁸And thus the paths of those on earth
were set right,
and people were taught what pleases
you,
and were saved by wisdom." (NRSVACE)

I would suggest that wisdom literature influenced Jesus in the substance of and the way he taught, but also the Beloved Disciple who learned from him, and we see the results.

WEEK NINE

GATHERING DISCUSSION OUTLINE

A. Open session in prayer.

B. View video for this week's readings.

C. What general impressions and thoughts do you have after considering the video, readings, and the daily writings on these Scriptures?

D. Discuss questions based on the daily readings.

    1. **KEY OBSERVATION:** In one sense, what we have in the Farewell Discourses is the teaching of Jesus that is most directly relevant to Christians.

    DISCUSSION QUESTION: What is the teaching in the Farewell Discourses intended to do?

    2. **KEY OBSERVATION:** Noteworthy about the character of the material in the Farewell Discourses is that it assumes that the world is going to require convincing to believe in Jesus.

    DISCUSSION QUESTION: What needs to happen to a person in order to be convinced of the gospel?

    3. **KEY OBSERVATION:** The early church was a missionary movement that also did discipleship and nurturing.

    DISCUSSION QUESTION: How does the church (in most places) of the twenty-first century compare to the early church in this regard?

4. **KEY OBSERVATION:** The Holy Spirit has rightly been called God's secret agent, or better said, the secret agent of Jesus himself, who sent the Spirit to the church. Sometimes people treat the Spirit as if he were a mere power or presence rather than a person.

   DISCUSSION QUESTION: What is the role of the Holy Spirit? What have you learned about the Holy Spirit in this study?

5. **KEY OBSERVATION:** One of the major terms used to describe the church in the New Testament is *ekklesia*, which refers to a called-out group of people. It was originally used in reference to the Greek democratic assembly.

   DISCUSSION QUESTION: Why do you think the New Testament writers chose this term to describe the church?

E. What facts and information presented in the commentary portion of the lesson help you understand the weekly Scripture?

F. Close session with prayer.

WEEK TEN

John 18:28–19:38

The Death of Jesus

INTRODUCTION

In the Gospel of John there is no Jewish trial. There is a hearing before the high priest(s), a threefold denial of Christ by Peter, and the handing over of Jesus to the Roman authorities. There is in general a strong emphasis on the Roman involvement in this whole process of arrest, trial, and then execution. Indeed, uniquely in this gospel, at John 18:3, we hear of a whole *speiran* of soldiers coming with the priestly officials and Judas to take Jesus into custody. This Greek word means a military, a technical term for either a maniple or a cohort of Roman soldiers—if the latter six hundred soldiers, if the former two hundred soldiers. Picture two hundred soldiers in the Garden of Gethsemane taking Jesus captive. This whole narrative quite literally suggests Roman over-kill. The real focus of the narrative, however, is the trial before Pilate, which is masterfully told. We will have some things to say about Pilate in the commentary notes. Pilate was not really a man concerned about justice for Jews; indeed he was famously anti-Semitic and not even wanting to cooperate with Jewish authorities. Knowing a bit about Pilate's character and previous actions help paint a clearer picture of what is going on in our narrative for this week.

It is clear that the Evangelist has taken great pains to set up this narrative carefully and dramatically. Not surprisingly, there are seven scenes to this story (the perfect number, of course) just as there were seven signs and seven "I am" sayings. The following analysis owes much to Fred Craddock, Bandy distinguished professor of preaching and New Testament emeritus in the Candler School of Theology at Emory University.

Scene One: Pilate is outside. He tries to discern the charge against Jesus and would like to pass the buck back to the Jewish officials (18:29–32).

Scene Two: Pilate is inside. He questions Jesus about the nature of kingship and truth. He is sarcastic and philosophical but does not understand Jesus (18:33–38a).

Scene Three: Pilate is outside. He declares Jesus innocent and offers his release according to the Paschal custom, but the crowd asks for Barabbas instead (18:38b–40).

Scene Four: Pilate is inside. Jesus is scourged and mocked (19:1–3).

Scene Five: Pilate is outside. He displays for public shaming the beaten, but royally attired Jesus. But this mockery doesn't satisfy the crowd or the officials. Indeed, it only increases the clamor for Jesus' crucifixion (19:4–7).

Scene Six: Pilate is inside. He is frightened and takes the position of a bully, waving his power and authority in Jesus' face, but Jesus calmly says Pilate would have no power or authority if God hadn't granted it to him (19:8–11).

Scene Seven: Pilate is outside. A last-ditch attempt to release Jesus fails, and Pilate is pressured into officially decreeing execution, while some Jews are maneuvered into renouncing their own right to have a king (19:12–16). What follows this is the judicial execution of Jesus on a Roman cross.

The Johannine presentation of the crucifixion is different from the Synoptics in various ways, not least in that we are told Jesus' mother is standing beneath the cross along with two other Marys and the Beloved Disciple. This would contradict the portrayal in the Synoptics, unless of course the Beloved Disciple is not one of the Twelve, but rather, a Judean disciple, probably Lazarus. In any case, Jesus is depicted as being in control of the whole situation even while on the cross. He carries his own cross (no mention of Simon of Cyrene) and when it is time for him to go, he simply says, "It is finished." As with the rest of this gospel, nothing happens by pure accident or luck, and no detail of the account is unimportant.

ONE

The King and the Governor

John 18:28–39 *Then the Jewish leaders took Jesus from Caiaphas to the palace of the Roman governor. By now it was early morning, and to avoid ceremonial uncleanness they did not enter the palace, because they wanted* to be able to eat the Passover. [29]So Pilate came out to them and asked, "What charges are you bringing against this man?"

[30]"If he were not a criminal," they replied, "we would not have handed him over to you." [31]Pilate said, "Take him yourselves and judge him by your own law." "But we have no right to execute anyone," they objected. [32]This took place to fulfill what Jesus had said about the kind of death he was going to die. [33]Pilate then went back inside the palace, summoned Jesus and asked him, "Are you the king of the Jews?" [34]"Is that your own idea," Jesus asked, "or did others talk to you about me?" [35]"Am I a Jew?" Pilate replied. "Your own people and chief priests handed you over to me. What is it you have done?" [36]Jesus said, "My kingdom is not of this world. If it were, my servants would fight to prevent my arrest by the Jewish leaders. But now my kingdom is from another place." [37]"You are a king, then!" said Pilate. Jesus answered, "You say that I am a king. In fact, the reason I was born and came into the world is to testify to the truth. Everyone on the side of truth listens to me." [38]"What is truth?" retorted Pilate. With this he went out again to the Jews gathered there and said, "I find no basis for a charge against him. [39]But it is your custom for me to release to you one prisoner at the time of the Passover. Do you want me to release 'the king of the Jews'?"

Understanding the Word. The account we have in this gospel reflects detailed knowledge of the exact legal situation of Jews under the direct Roman rule of a Roman governor. Above all else, in such provinces, the Romans jealously guarded the right of capital punishment and would not allow subordinate local officials to execute people. Of course, from time to time, vigilante justice happened anyway (e.g., in the case of the stoning of Stephen). But the Jewish officials, chiefly Caiaphas, who was then high priest in AD 30, wanted Jesus publicly dealt with so a public shaming would result, and he did not want to be responsible for it, as he knew many Jews thought highly of Jesus. And so, he must have thought handing Jesus over to an often violent and vicious Pilate would be the perfect solution to his dilemma. As it turned out, he got more than he bargained for when he handed Jesus over. Pilate seems to have smelled a rat and had no great desire to give the Jewish officials what they wanted. Indeed, he would have rather tweaked their noses and released Jesus, just to show who was really in control in Judea. But other factors came into play.

The narrative begins with great irony. The officials don't scruple to hand a fellow Jew over to the brutal Romans, but they won't enter the Roman *praetorium* (probably an adaptation of Herod's palace in Jerusalem, and so not at the Antonio Fortress) for fear of contracting uncleanness, which would mess up their Passover party. Of course, Passover was the celebration of the liberation from bondage under Pharaoh, so it is highly ironic that the officials don't see the contradiction between that celebration and binding Jesus and handing him over to the local Roman pharaoh.

Pilate quite properly asks what charges are brought against Jesus. No one really wanted to have an execution during Passover, so this is a rush job, but Pilate is in no mood to be rushed into an execution. He knows it will just inflame some of the Jews present for the Passover feast. At first the officials stonewall Pilate by saying, "If he were not a criminal, we would not have handed him over to you." What one needs to know about this situation is that there were really only two crimes that brought the punishment of crucifixion normally—sedition (claiming illegally to be a king or having governing authority and so undermining existing Roman authority), and leading a slave revolt (another form of sedition). This is why Pilate questions Jesus as he does. He is not interested in Jewish religious squabbles about blasphemy against some Jewish law that he has no interest in upholding. None. His job is to keep the peace and execute Roman law.

At first Pilate suggests that the Jewish officials take Jesus and judge him by their own law, but they tip their hand by saying, "All very well, but we can't execute the man." In other words, this is a capital case, a serious crime against the state. It is interesting that we are told that the officials said this and thereby unconsciously fulfilled the way Jesus prophesied he would be executed. Even the Jewish officials are used by God to work out his plan.

Pilate goes back inside and comes right to the point—"Are you the king of the Jews?" You will notice he doesn't ask if he was the Jewish messiah, or a great prophet or the like. He did not care if Jesus was some other kind of anointed holy man, but if he claimed to be what Herod the Great had previously claimed, there was a clear conflict with Roman law. When a province had a Roman governor, he was the highest official, and anyone who claimed to be a king was usurping the governor's power and authority.

As usual, Jesus answers a question with a question—"Is that your own idea, or did someone put that idea into your head?" Jesus is not really cooperating with this whole travesty of justice. Of course, even here there is irony. Jesus really *is* and claims to be the King of the Jews (see the triumphal entry story), and so, by Roman law, it would be just to execute him as a usurper and revolutionary. Pilate is insulted and perhaps surprised by Jesus' retort and spits out, "Am I a Jew?" An insulting suggestion to an anti-Semitic Roman. He surmises that Jesus must have done something really bad to cause his handing over by the Jewish officials, but he hasn't really figured out what yet.

Jesus responds that his kingdom is not of this world, which is why his followers do not fight to prevent his capture. Pilate however seizes on the word *kingdom*, and says, "Aha! So you are claiming to be a king!" Jesus is evasive—"That's what you would call me." Jesus is not interested in labels, but in the truth, and he says he came into the world to testify to it. Cynical Pilate sneers and asks, "And what exactly is truth?" Again, there is irony because the Truth is standing right in front of Pilate. When Pilate gets no further answer from interrogating Jesus, he goes out, probably thinking Jesus is another Jewish madman, and says he finds no reason to charge Jesus under Roman law. And then he slyly suggests that since there is a custom of releasing someone at Passover, perhaps he could show *clementia* (clemency) and do this, which might make him look good in the eyes of some Jews. With a sneer he asks, "Do you want me to release the so-called king of the Jews?"

1. What is your impression of Pilate from this episode? Is he really interested in justice for Jesus?

2. How would you read Jesus' responses to Pilate? Is he being evasive?

3. What do you make of the Jewish officials' role in all this?

TWO

The Son of Abba and the Son of God

John 18:40–19:7 *They shouted back, "No, not him! Give us Barabbas!" Now Barabbas had taken part in an uprising. ¹Then Pilate took Jesus and had him* *flogged. ²The soldiers twisted together a crown of thorns and put it on his head. They clothed him in a purple robe ³and went up to him again and again, saying, "Hail, king of the Jews!" And they slapped him in the face. ⁴Once more Pilate came out and said to the Jews gathered there, "Look, I am bringing him out to you to let you know that I find no basis for a charge against him." ⁵When Jesus came out wearing the crown of thorns and the purple robe, Pilate said to them, "Here is the man!" ⁶As soon as the chief priests and their officials saw him, they shouted, "Crucify! Crucify!" But Pilate answered, "You take him and crucify him. As for me, I find no basis for a charge against him." ⁷The Jewish leaders insisted, "We have a law, and according to that law he must die, because he claimed to be the Son of God."*

Understanding the Word. The name Barabbas is an Aramaic name, and it literally means "son of Abba," that is, "son of his father." This contrasts nicely with the end of the story, where we hear that Jesus claims to be the Son of God. Now, Barabbas is a revolutionary, and while we are at it, the two men on the cross beside Jesus were not thieves. Theft was not a capital crime under Roman law. No, those two men are revolutionary bandits just like Barabbas, who had taken part in an uprising against the Romans, and Jesus himself will be crucified as some kind of revolutionary because he claims to be a king. But the claim that he was the Son of God is more alarming still, not least because Pilate would take the phrase "a son of the gods" to be like the claims of the emperor, not merely a governor or a petty king.

The flogging of Jesus, and the crown of thorns in this case, should not be seen as part of the process of execution. Pilate has not decided to execute Jesus. Instead he is hoping that a simple flogging of the madman, and a public shaming, will be sufficient, and he can be done with this sordid affair. No such luck. After the flogging Pilate says, "Look, I find no basis to execute Jesus. Behold this pitiful man!" (The implication being, how could he be a king or a real threat?) When the Jewish officials see this, they shout to crucify him. Pilate in disgust says, "You take him and crucify him!" But then the officials play a further trump card, saying, "We do have a law that says he should die, as he claimed to be the Son of God." (But as they said before, they don't have the authorization to kill him). This claim frightens Pilate. Maybe there is more to Jesus than meets the eye. Another inquisition ensues.

1. Why do you think Pilate flogs and then tries to release Jesus?

2. What do you make of the ironic juxtaposition of Barabbas, a real violent revolutionary, and Jesus, a nonviolent revolutionary? Which was the bigger threat to Roman power and authority?

3. Why would Jesus' claim to be the Son of God frighten Pilate?

THREE

No King but Caesar

John 19:8–16a *When Pilate heard this, he was even more afraid, ⁹and he went back inside the palace. "Where do you come from?" he asked Jesus, but Jesus gave him no answer. ¹⁰"Do you refuse to speak to me?" Pilate said. "Don't you realize I have power either to free you or to crucify you?" ¹¹Jesus answered, "You would have no power over me if it were not given to you from above. Therefore the one who handed me over to you is guilty of a greater sin." ¹²From then on, Pilate tried to set Jesus free, but the Jewish leaders kept shouting, "If you let this man go, you are no friend of Caesar. Anyone who claims to be a king opposes Caesar." ¹³When Pilate heard this, he brought Jesus out and sat down on the judge's seat at a place known as the Stone Pavement (which in Aramaic is Gabbatha). ¹⁴It was the day of Preparation of the Passover; it was about noon.*

"Here is your king," Pilate said to the Jews. ¹⁵But they shouted, "Take him away! Take him away! Crucify him!" "Shall I crucify your king?" Pilate asked. "We have no king but Caesar," the chief priests answered. ¹⁶Finally Pilate handed him over to them to be crucified.

Understanding the Word. Pilate returns to the palace afraid. He asks Jesus where he comes from, and by the way, this whole exchange had to be in Greek. Pilate would not have known Aramaic or Hebrew, and Jesus was unlikely to have learned Latin. Now this question is the buzzword question that permeates this whole gospel—knowing who Jesus is depends on knowing where he came from; namely, he came from heaven as the only begotten Son of God.

This time Jesus simply refuses to answer the question, which Pilate takes as an insult and so Pilate threatens Jesus, saying, "Don't you know

I have the power to crucify you or set you free?" Jesus doesn't flinch. He suggests that Pilate has only derived authority, and it was ultimately not given to him by Caesar, but by God. Jesus suggests that since Pilate is flying blind in this matter, those who handed him over are guilty of a bigger sin, for they know more of who Jesus is, and what the real situation is. This answer must have pleased Pilate, as we are told that from then on in this tug-of-war, he tries to release Jesus, but it is not to be. The Jewish officials play their final trump card saying if Pilate releases Jesus, then he will be no friend of Caesar. Now, *amicus Caesaris* was an official status that Pilate desperately wanted to keep. This meant being on the emperor's good side, in line for better appointments later. But if the Jewish officials went to the Emperor Tiberius and complained about Pilate, this might get him in hot water, because already he had caused some trouble in the province of Judea, and the emperor was watching (cf. Luke 13:1). He wanted the Pax Romana to prevail, even in Judea. So Pilate brings out his curule chair, the judgment seat, and sits down at a spot called Gabbatha, and again presents Jesus to the crowd, in essence giving them a choice about his punishment. They shout to crucify him, and now, finally, Pilate had been outmaneuvered, so he says in anger, "Shall I crucify your king?" The crowd infamously says, "We have no king but Caesar"—a complete renunciation of the patrimony of the Jews and their Davidic heritage. It was noon on the day of Preparation for the Passover, and the real Passover lamb was about to be slaughtered on the appropriate day. It is not clear who "them" is at the end of this segment, but presumably it means his Roman soldiers who worked closely with the Jewish officials (some of those perhaps who had taken Jesus captive in the garden the previous night).

1. What motivated Pilate to finally have Jesus crucified?

2. It is important to realize that not all Jews present wanted Jesus crucified. This is not really an attempt to blacken all Jews and make them directly responsible for Jesus' death. He was executed by Romans. Why, then, do you think that Christians have wrongly blamed the Jews in general for centuries?

3. What did it mean to be "a friend of Caesar"?

FOUR

The Title and the Robe

John 19:16b–24 *So the soldiers took charge of Jesus.* ¹⁷*Carrying his own cross, he went out to the place of the Skull (which in Aramaic is called Golgotha).* ¹⁸*There they crucified him, and with him two others—one on each side and Jesus in the middle.* ¹⁹*Pilate had a notice prepared and fastened to the cross. It read:* JESUS OF NAZARETH, THE KING OF THE JEWS. ²⁰*Many of the Jews read this sign, for the place where Jesus was crucified was near the city, and the sign was written in Aramaic, Latin and Greek.* ²¹*The chief priests of the Jews protested to Pilate, "Do not write 'The King of the Jews,' but that this man claimed to be king of the Jews."* ²²*Pilate answered, "What I have written, I have written."* ²³*When the soldiers crucified Jesus, they took his clothes, dividing them into four shares, one for each of them, with the undergarment remaining. This garment was seamless, woven in one piece from top to bottom.* ²⁴*"Let's not tear it," they said to one another. "Let's decide by lot who will get it." This happened that the scripture might be fulfilled that said, "They divided my clothes among them and cast lots for my garment."*

So this is what the soldiers did.

Understanding the Word. The *titulus*, or placard that would be hung on the cross, indicated the crime for which the person was being executed. It is important to note that Jesus is crucified for being "king of the Jews," not messiah or prophet, but rather the universal political term—king. The title is written in three languages: Latin, Greek, and either Hebrew or Aramaic, probably the latter. Aramaic was sometimes called the Hebrew tongue, especially in Judea because this is the language that Jews from Judea had come home from Babylon speaking. Aramaic is a sister tongue to Hebrew. There is a further squabble over the titulus. The priests want a modification so that it would merely say that Jesus *claimed* to be the king of the Jews, but Pilate does not cave in. He says it's too late for that, a legal verdict has been rendered: "What I have written, I have written." And so the irony of the whole story continues. The King of the Jews is both wrongly and rightly executed for being "the king of the Jews"—wrongly because his kingdom is not of this world, rightly because he really was the King of the Jews, and that had political implications.

As we have said, in this gospel the spotlight is on Jesus. He carries his own cross, there is no verbal exchange with the other people being executed (they are barely mentioned in passing), and the soldiers gamble over Jesus' inner garment, a more expensive seamless robe. There is historical evidence that executioners had a right to claim property of those whom they executed. The Evangelist, however, wants to stress that here is another little detail that fulfills Scripture, in this case Psalm 22:18. It is interesting that while we do not have the cry of dereliction by Jesus from the cross in John—i.e., "My God, my God, why have you forsaken me?" (found in Matthew and Mark), it is also a quote from that same Psalm 22. It is clear that that whole psalm was read messianically as a clue to how to make sense of Jesus' death on the cross. I would encourage you to go back and read the psalm at this point. One final note: the curtain in Herod's temple was seamless, and in the Synoptics we hear about it being ripped from top to bottom at the point of Jesus' death, which is seen as a divine act and omen. Here Jesus, who has said that his body is the real temple, has the covering of his holy self taken, and it too is seamless, and the soldiers say, "Let's not tear it." This is an interesting point and counterpoint when you compare the Synoptic and Johannine stories about the crucifixion.

1. Why do you think the Evangelist focuses on what he does in this telling of the demise of Jesus, making various unique points not found elsewhere?

2. Crucifixion was normally in the nude, as part of the total shaming of the victim, and this account suggests that the soldiers gambled for Jesus' undergarment. Why do you think artists have always depicted Jesus as at least having a loincloth on when he hung on the cross?

3. What blame should be placed on these soldiers, if any, for following orders and doing their job?

FIVE

The Last Will and Testament of the King

John 19:25–37 *Near the cross of Jesus stood his mother, his mother's sister, Mary the wife of Clopas, and Mary Magdalene. [26]When Jesus saw his mother there, and the disciple whom he loved standing nearby, he said to her, "Woman, here is your son," [27]and to the disciple, "Here is your mother." From that time on, this disciple took her into his home. [28]Later, knowing that everything had now been finished, and so that Scripture would be fulfilled, Jesus said, "I am thirsty." [29]A jar of wine vinegar was there, so they soaked a sponge in it, put the sponge on a stalk of the hyssop plant, and lifted it to Jesus' lips. [30]When he had received the drink, Jesus said, "It is finished." With that, he bowed his head and gave up his spirit. [31]Now it was the day of Preparation, and the next day was to be a special Sabbath. Because the Jewish leaders did not want the bodies left on the crosses during the Sabbath, they asked Pilate to have the legs broken and the bodies taken down. [32]The soldiers therefore came and broke the legs of the first man who had been crucified with Jesus, and then those of the other. [33]But when they came to Jesus and found that he was already dead, they did not break his legs. [34]Instead, one of the soldiers pierced Jesus' side with a spear, bringing a sudden flow of blood and water. [35]The man who saw it has given testimony, and his testimony is true. He knows that he tells the truth, and he testifies so that you also may believe. [36]These things happened so that the scripture would be fulfilled: "Not one of his bones will be broken," [37]and, as another scripture says, "They will look on the one they have pierced."*

Understanding the Word. At the cross, according to the Synoptics, were none of the Twelve, and only women are mentioned. In John, we have Mary (the mother of Jesus), Mary (the wife of Clopas), the sister of Jesus' mother, and Mary Magdalene (the leader of the female disciples), with the Beloved Disciple nearby. There is evidence that a person could make a last will and testament on behalf of his loved ones even from a cross, and it would be valid. In this case, Jesus doesn't distribute his property (the Romans had already confiscated that), but he bequeaths his mother to the Beloved Disciple, and vice versa. He says nothing to the other two Marys present. What is shocking about this is that Jesus' mother is not entrusted into the care of Jesus' brothers or sisters, but rather into the care of Jesus' most beloved disciple, whom I take to be Lazarus. Now, this makes good sense of the story because we are told the Beloved Disciple takes Mary into his own home, which would be nearby in Bethany. This also makes sense in light of Acts 1:14 when Mary is still in Jerusalem praying at the time of Pentecost, some fifty days later. Had the Beloved Disciple been a Galilean disciple, he would have gone back home to Galilee after seeing Jesus in Jerusalem (see John 21), and this includes the Zebedees, who are finally mentioned in John 21, but only in passing. Furthermore, we learned earlier in John 18 that the "other disciple" (i.e., the Beloved Disciple) had an all-access pass into the high priest's house, which is unlikely if the Beloved Disciple was a Galilean like Peter. This may explain as well why he is allowed to be near the cross. He is known to the soldiers who work with the priestly authorities.

Jesus' mother is once more addressed as "woman" as in John 2. And now the Beloved Disciple is said to be her son, and she his mother. This is Jesus bringing a member of his physical family into the family of faith as the last act of his earthly ministry. Undoubtedly this is something he deeply wanted to happen. Later, Jesus would appear to his brother James (see 1 Corinthians 15), which presumably explains why the brothers are also present in the upper room, praying before Pentecost (see Acts 1:14). Unbelief has given way to belief, in the light of the resurrection and appearances of Jesus, even to James.

At verse 28, Jesus quotes Psalm 22:18, indicating another fulfillment of Scripture from that psalm. On the surface there would appear to be a contradiction between the Synoptic and the Johannine portrayals here, but there is not. What Jesus is offered in John is wine vinegar on a sponge—the Gatorade of their day. In the Synoptics Jesus is offered sour wine, a narcotic that would dull the pain a little bit, but actually prolong the agony. This Jesus refuses, as he doesn't want to prolong the agony. After all, atonement is not about the amount of suffering; it's about the death of the lamb. After drinking this, Jesus declares all has been fulfilled and finished, and he bows his head and dies. We are spared any gruesome descriptions of the final agonies. Jesus is depicted as dying with dignity, and in control to the end.

Originally, the Jewish officials had wanted to wait until after the Passover to deal with Jesus and others, presumably not wanting to spoil the Passover celebrations, but it was not to be. So now, as the sun had already begun to sink (Jesus died at the ninth hour, which is 3 p.m.), there was a need to get the execution process over with quickly, and the bodies off the crosses. There is, therefore, the request to have the legs of the victims broken so they could not hold their chest cavities up any longer, and would quickly die of asphyxiation. In the case of Jesus, however, this proved unnecessary, as Jesus had already died, and to make sure of it, a soldier pierced him in the chest cavity with a spear, water and blood flowing forth from his side. In later Christian exegesis this was seen as emblematic or symbolic of the sacraments, both baptism and the Lord's Supper, but here it is simply an indication Jesus was truly, fully mortal, and truly died.

At verse 35 we have an important statement: "The man who saw it has given testimony, and his testimony is true. He knows that he tells the truth, and he testifies so that you also may believe." This should be compared to the purpose statement in John 20:31. Notice the present tense here. When we get to John 21 however, the Beloved Disciple is spoken of in the past tense, and we hear the community say, "We know his testimony is true." In both cases, the reference is to the Beloved Disciple, and here we have a clue to this gospel. This gospel is chiefly the memoirs of the Beloved Disciple, which according to John 21 he actually wrote down. This means he was a literate man, among other things. When he wrote down his testimony, he was still alive, hence the statement here in verse 35. The final editor (whom I take to be John of Patmos acting on behalf of the community after the Beloved Disciple's death), edited the material, arranged things, added editorial comments required for an audience in Ephesus, and so on. Thankfully, we have this gospel. It is an eyewitness testimony, later edited by a writer of another New Testament book, Revelation. And since he was finally responsible for its gospel form, it was attributed to John. But it was not John's personal testimony. We may ask finally, Why the stress on eyewitness testimony at this juncture? The answer, in part, is surely to reassure that Jesus was indeed genuinely human and truly died (not merely swooned), and so atonement was truly accomplished, finished.

There are two further final fulfillments of Scripture seen in all this: "Not one of his bones will be broken," which seems to be a combination citation of Psalm 34:20, Exodus 12:46, and Numbers 9:12; and "They will look on the one they have pierced," which is a reference to Zechariah 12:10. Again it was critical to demonstrate that almost everything that happened on the last day of Jesus' life happened according to the Scriptures precisely because no one was looking for a crucified messiah. No one. Not even Jesus' family, not even the disciples, not even the Beloved Disciple who saw it right to the end. Understanding came after the fact.

1. What do you make of Jesus' last will and testament?

2. In what sense would Mary be the mother of the Beloved Disciple, and the Beloved Disciple be her son?

3. Why did Jesus say, "It is finished" as he died?

COMMENTARY NOTES

General Comments. Crucifixion was, without question, one of the most hideous ways to die ever invented by humankind. It was not a well-known or frequent punishment, so far as we can tell, before the time of the Roman Empire. But the Romans used it in abundance as part of their shock-and-awe campaign to break people's spirits while taking over their land. Even Romans called it the extreme punishment, and Cicero went so far as to say it shouldn't be mentioned in polite company, never mind witnessed!

Crucifixion did not always involve nails; sometimes it involved ropes, and sometimes, at night, crucifixion victims who were tied up were rescued from their crosses. When Romans wanted to make sure no escape was possible, especially in high-profile cases, nails were used, usually three nails—one through the holes in the top of the feet (one foot stacked on the other), and one through each wrist, again where the hole in the wrist joint can be felt. All those medieval paintings of Jesus nailed in the palm of his hands are clearly by people who had never witnessed a crucifixion.

The cross for a crucifixion could take more than one shape. It could be like a giant T, it could be like a large X, and finally it could also be like a small *t*, with a top piece. It seems likely that Jesus' cross was like the latter, since a titulus had to be nailed somewhere specifying the crime committed. Whichever form it took, it involved extreme pain, and normally the victims who had been nailed to crosses, especially after flogging, did not last for long. Jesus appears to have been on the cross only a few hours before expiring in mid-afternoon under a Judean sun. Sometimes there would be a little piece of wood in the middle of the cross where the victim could occasionally rest his backside. This was not put on the cross as an act of compassion, but rather to prolong the agony. The victim mostly needed to be erect to breathe properly, and when they wore out, they began gasping for breath.

The function of crucifixion was not simply execution, but public humiliation of the victim and the ruination of his name, reputation, and honor. We must remember this is an honor-and-shame culture, and public shaming was often viewed as a fate worse than death. In this case crucifixion involved both. No one in antiquity would have engaged in the grisly practice of wearing little images of crosses around their neck. That would have been the equivalent of wearing little gold electric chairs or gallows around their necks. It was a considerable mystery to most ancient Jews and pagans how a deity could get himself crucified. Crucifixion should have scotched the rumor that Jesus was anything special at all, never mind the divine Son of God. We need to take seriously what Paul says: "We preach Christ crucified: a [*scandalon*] stumbling block to Jews and foolishness to Gentiles"

(1 Cor. 1:23). He was right. There was no sugarcoating a death on a cross. Most would have seen it as something hideous and ridiculous, not something sacred.

Day 1. If we had any doubts about the true character of Pilate (who eventually ended up in exile after serving in Judea until about AD 37), Josephus sets the record straight. Here is a sample story about his brutal practices and insensitivity to the Jews.

Flavius Josephus, *The Jewish War*, 2.175–77:

> On a later occasion he provoked a fresh uproar by expending upon the construction of an aqueduct the sacred treasure known as Corbonas; the water was brought from a distance of seventy kilometers. Indignant at this proceeding, the populace formed a ring round the tribunal of Pilate, then on a visit to Jerusalem, and besieged him with angry clamor. He, foreseeing the tumult, had interspersed among the crowd a troop of his soldiers, armed but disguised in civilian dress, with orders not to use their swords, but to beat any rioters with cudgels. He now from his tribunal gave the agreed signal. Large numbers of the Jews perished, some from the blows which they received, others trodden to death by their companions in the ensuing flight. Cowed by the fate of the victims, the multitude was reduced to silence.

WEEK TEN

GATHERING DISCUSSION OUTLINE

A. Open session in prayer.

B. View video for this week's readings.

C. What general impressions and thoughts do you have after considering the video, readings, and the daily writings on these Scriptures?

D. Discuss questions based on the daily readings.

1. **KEY OBSERVATION:** One of the major factors to keep steadily in view as we evaluate the trial and death of Jesus is that many ancient people believed that how a person died most revealed his character. And crucifixion was not seen as a noble way to die.

   DISCUSSION QUESTION: What was the function of crucifixion? In what light is crucifixion seen as positive and redemptive?

2. **KEY OBSERVATION:** The trial before Pilate is brilliantly presented in the Fourth Gospel, and the overall effect is to portray Pilate doing everything he can to avoid giving the Jewish authorities what they want—the crucifixion of Jesus.

   DISCUSSION QUESTION: What motivated Pilate to finally have Jesus crucified?

3. **KEY OBSERVATION:** The loyalty of women to Jesus, right to the end of his life, is touching and historically believable. They could be there at the cross because the soldiers would not see them as a threat.

DISCUSSION QUESTION: Why would the soldiers not see the women as a threat?

4. **KEY OBSERVATION:** It is important to realize that not all Jews present wanted Jesus crucified. This is not really an attempt to blacken all Jews and make them directly responsible for Jesus' death. He was executed by Romans.

   DISCUSSION QUESTION: Why, then, do you think that Christians have wrongly blamed the Jews in general for centuries?

5. **KEY OBSERVATION:** It was critical to demonstrate that almost everything that happened on the last day of Jesus' life happened according to the Scriptures precisely because no one was looking for a crucified messiah.

   DISCUSSION QUESTION: Read the following passages. How are these Scriptures fulfilled in the crucifixion of Jesus: Psalm 34:20; Exodus 12:43–46; Numbers 9:12; Zechariah 12:10; and Psalm 22:18.

E. What facts and information presented in the commentary portion of the lesson help you understand the weekly Scripture?

F. Close session with prayer.

WEEK ELEVEN

John 20:1–31

Jesus' Resurrection and Appearances

INTRODUCTION

In the first portion of John 20, we have a narrative that the famous British New Testament scholar C. H. Dodd once called the most self-authenticating example of any of the appearance stories. By this he meant that no one in Jesus' patriarchal culture would make up a story about an emotional woman, deep in grief, being the first and reliable witness to see the risen Jesus. The testimony of women was not generally seen as valid in antiquity, and certainly not in most courts. You don't start a new world religion by telling stories about women being the chief witnesses to the death and resurrection of your hero, not if you want to do effective evangelism in a world that had a low view of women, and most of which believed dead men tell no tales, and certainly do not rise again!

It is rightly observed that while the Passion Narratives in all four Gospels record basically the same events, when we get to Easter, the accounts vary remarkably. Mark, as we have it, ending at Mark 16:8, has no account of anyone meeting the risen Jesus, but this is likely because we have lost the original ending. Matthew has appearances both in Judea and Galilee, but they differ from the appearances in Luke. Luke has only appearances in Judea, including a totally unique appearance on the road to Emmaus. The appearances in John match up in some respects with those in Matthew, and to a lesser degree in Luke. In particular, the appearance to Mary Magdalene (which is told in long form in John 20) seems to be told in short form in Matthew 28:8–10. The reason for all of these different stories is because Jesus seems to have appeared in a variety of places to a variety of people, sometimes in groups, occasionally to individuals, and so the gospel writers picked and chose how they would end the Easter story, whereas with the trial and death of Jesus there was only one sequence of events for them all to report.

In John 20 we have the visit to the empty tomb, first by Mary, then by Peter and the Beloved Disciple; the appearance of Jesus to Mary; two different appearances, a week apart, to the male disciples in the upper room; and a conclusion to the gospel with a purpose statement. John 21 stands out from this clearly as an appendix, and it may have been added at a later date, say, after the Beloved Disciple and Peter had both died, in part to explain such things.

ONE
Tomb Raiders

John 20:1–10 *Early on the first day of the week, while it was still dark, Mary Magdalene went to the tomb and saw that the stone had been removed from the entrance. ²So she came running to Simon Peter and the other disciple, the one Jesus loved, and said, "They have taken the Lord out of the tomb, and we don't know where they have put him!" ³So Peter and the other disciple started for the tomb. ⁴Both were running, but the other disciple outran Peter and reached the tomb first. ⁵He bent over and looked in at the strips of linen lying there but did not go in. ⁶Then Simon Peter came along behind him and went straight into the tomb. He saw the strips of linen lying there, ⁷as well as the cloth that had been wrapped around Jesus' head. The cloth was still lying in its place, separate from the linen. ⁸Finally the other disciple, who had reached the tomb first, also went inside. He saw and believed. ⁹(They still did not understand from Scripture that Jesus had to rise from the dead.) ¹⁰Then the disciples went back to where they were staying.*

Understanding the Word. Whatever else one can say about the empty tomb of Jesus stories, none of the Evangelists saw this as what generated the appearance stories and belief in the resurrection of Jesus. An empty tomb could be explained in various ways, and indeed Mary Magdalene in our text seems to assume someone has taken the body—a tomb raider. The empty tomb left a big question mark in the minds of the disciples, even the Beloved Disciple, as we shall see. It did not lead to Easter faith and did not transform anyone. Instead it led to dismay, enhanced grief, puzzlement, fear, and the like. Without supernatural explanation and intervention, we might still be wondering.

The initial story in this chapter focuses on Mary Magdalene. She reports to the male disciples that they don't know where Jesus had been taken, which suggests several women had gone to the tomb with her, as the Synoptics indicate. The Fourth Evangelist simply decided to focus on the experience of Mary Magdalene. She has not been a character in the Fourth Gospel before being mentioned at the cross in John 19. Her real name was probably Miryam, named after the Old Testament prophetess, and she came from a considerable fishing village on the northwest corner of the Sea of Galilee, called Migdal, from which the name Magdalene comes. (This town has been recently excavated, revealing a remarkable synagogue and a large fish factory.) Miryam should not necessarily be depicted as a woman from a tiny fishing village.

In the Johannine telling of the story, Miryam goes to the tomb, finds the stone rolled away and no body, and immediately rushes off and reports to the representatives of the Galilean disciples (Peter) and of the Judean disciples (the Beloved Disciple, who is here called both "the other [main] disciple" as well as "the one Jesus loved"). Her report is simply: "They have [she does not say who] taken the Lord out of the tomb, and we don't know where they have put him!" Peter and the Beloved Disciple go to investigate and, lo and behold, find that her testimony is accurate. What is especially important to note is that *none of the canonical Gospels record anyone as witnessing Jesus' actual rising from the dead. They record the aftermath of that event—an empty tomb and various appearances.* Only in the much later apocryphal Gospel of Peter do we have a tale about someone witnessing Jesus coming out of the tomb (and being followed by a cross the size of Walmart!). The canonical Gospels are circumspect in the way they tell these stories; they are careful not to say more than they have concrete testimony to back up. Nobody, so far as we know (unless the angels count), saw Jesus rise from the dead. They saw the results of that miracle. It is worth adding at this juncture that early Jews who believed in resurrection believed it was something that happened to a human body, to a corpse, transforming it. They would not have suggested it was a purely spiritual experience, or that the body that resulted was not a material body. That is not what early Jews believed about resurrection.

Neither Peter nor the Beloved Disciple, when they get to the tomb of Jesus, see angels. All they see is grave clothes. Notice that the Beloved

Disciple gets there first, perhaps because being from the Jerusalem area, and probably knowing Joseph of Arimathea, he knew where the tomb was. The Beloved Disciple does not at first go into the tomb but sees the grave clothes, whereas Peter comes along behind him and has no hesitation in entering the tomb. Finally the Beloved Disciple enters as well, and we are told, "He saw and believed"—but believed what? The very next sentence says, "They still did not understand from Scripture that Jesus had to rise from the dead." I suspect what "he saw and believed" means is that the Beloved Disciple thought Jesus had been taken directly up into heaven, like Elijah before him. This would make sense of what he had heard earlier in the Farewell Discourses when Jesus talked about needing to return to the Father so he could send the Spirit. In other words, the Beloved Disciple does not appear to be an exception to the rule that it was only the appearances of Jesus that convinced people he had risen from the dead. Notice that the text does not add that suddenly the Beloved Disciple started praising God and making up Easter hymns. No, we are told they went quietly back to where they were staying.

1. What do you make of the empty tomb?

2. What do the grave clothes, rolled up neatly, suggest to you?

3. What do you think the Beloved Disciple believed about Jesus on the basis of the empty tomb?

TWO

Mary, Mary, Extraordinary

John 20:11–18 *Now Mary stood outside the tomb crying. As she wept, she bent over to look into the tomb* [12]*and saw two angels in white, seated where Jesus' body had been, one at the head and the other at the foot.* [13]*They asked her, "Woman, why are you crying?" "They have taken my Lord away," she said, "and I don't know where they have put him."* [14]*At this, she turned around and saw Jesus standing there, but she did not realize that it was Jesus.* [15]*He asked her, "Woman, why are you crying? Who is it you are looking for?"*

Thinking he was the gardener, she said, "Sir, if you have carried him away, tell me where you have put him, and I will get him." ¹⁶Jesus said to her, "Mary." She turned toward him and cried out in Aramaic, "Rabboni!" (which means "Teacher"). ¹⁷Jesus said, "Do not hold on to me, for I have not yet ascended to the Father. Go instead to my brothers and tell them, 'I am ascending to my Father and your Father, to my God and your God.'" ¹⁸Mary Magdalene went to the disciples with the news: "I have seen the Lord!" And she told them that he had said these things to her.

Understanding the Word. Mary had returned to the tomb with the male disciples, but she did not leave like them. She lingered at the tomb, weeping and mourning. So deep was her grief that even the appearance of two angels couldn't shake her out of her distraught state.

Angels in the biblical tradition are like neon signs saying, "God is at work here." They always presage or proclaim something is about to happen or has happened. I like to call them God's FedEx messengers. They do their job quickly and just as quickly disappear. In this case we have two angels, one at the head of the slab, one at the foot, as holy bookends signaling where the body had been. There was now a void between them, but it was not devoid of meaning. There may be two because in the Jewish tradition the truth of anything needed to be confirmed by at least two witnesses.

The angels ask Mary a question that seems totally unnecessary—"Woman, why are you crying?" But surely they know. Mary simply reiterates what she had said to the male disciples, "They have taken my Lord away, and I don't know where they have put him." If we put ourselves in her place for a moment, we need to remember that she had come to the tomb to perform her own memorial acts—with anointing oil and fresh linens. To her it must have seemed liked the final straw, the last possible degradation of someone whom she had followed and revered, that she was to be deprived of even being able to perform last rites for Jesus, or as we might say, to put one last wreath on the grave and say good-bye. This was the unkindest cut of all, the ultimate indignity and denigration of his memory. So she is naturally distraught.

Sensing someone approaching from outside the tomb, she turns away from the scene of where he had been laid and sees someone that in a moment she will assume is the gardener. Strangely, he asks her the very same thing the angels did—"Woman, why are you crying?" But then there is an additional question about a *who,* not a what (i.e., a corpse). "Who is it you are looking for?"

Her response doesn't mention Jesus by name, but she assumes the gardener will know who she's talking about: "Sir, if you have carried him away, tell me where you have put him, and I will get him." It is only at this juncture that we have the magical moment. Jesus calls Mary by name—"Miryam." Surely her heart leapt, recognizing finally the sound of his voice, and she responds, "Rabboni," which means "my master" or "teacher" in Aramaic. We are doubtless meant to remember what Jesus had said in the Good Shepherd discourse, "I know my sheep and they know the sound of my voice, and I call each one by name."

At this point, in her euphoria, Mary seizes Jesus, and he has to respond, "Don't cling to me," which is important because Jesus doesn't want her to think that she could just continue the relationship of the past with her rabboni. She must not cling to the Jesus of the past, as he is going to be with his Father, and not bodily present in a few more days. Instead Jesus commissions her to be the apostle to the apostles. He tells her to go tell the male disciples that he is ascending to his Father and their Father, his God and their God. And so Mary went on her way proclaiming, "I have seen the [risen] Lord,"—the very first Easter witness. It ought to be said that if Jesus can commission a woman to proclaim to the male apostles the first Easter message, there can't be anything wrong with having women preachers! She also told them what he asked her to tell them as well.

It probably doesn't need to be said, but this text makes clear that we are not (à la *The Da Vinci Code*) talking about the joyful reunion of husband and wife here. Mary does not say, "Husband, I'm so glad you're back; let's jump-start our marriage by reading a marriage renewal book!" Of course not. Mary was just Jesus' disciple, and she addresses him as her teacher.

1. What do you make of the angels in the tomb?

2. Why would Mary have been so distraught to find an empty tomb?

3. How do you feel about Jesus commissioning Mary to proclaim the first Easter message to the Twelve (or in this case the eleven, plus other male disciples like the Beloved Disciple)?

THREE

The First Sunday Night Appearance

John 20:19–23 *On the evening of that first day of the week, when the disciples were together, with the doors locked for fear of the Jewish leaders, Jesus came and stood among them and said, "Peace be with you!"* [20]*After he said this, he showed them his hands and side. The disciples were overjoyed when they saw the Lord.* [21]*Again Jesus said, "Peace be with you! As the Father has sent me, I am sending you."* [22]*And with that he breathed on them and said, "Receive the Holy Spirit.* [23]*If you forgive anyone's sins, their sins are forgiven; if you do not forgive them, they are not forgiven."*

Understanding the Word. The first thing to notice about this story is that the main disciples are still huddled behind locked doors, afraid of the Jewish officials. Apparently, the testimony of Mary was not received, and indeed, if you look at the Lukan account in Luke 24:11, we are told "But they did not believe the women, because their words seemed to them like nonsense." In other words, male chauvinism and prejudice had prevented the men from believing the good news. Only an appearance of Jesus himself could transform them from fearful to faith-filled.

Apparently, Jesus simply suddenly appears in their midst and says, "Shalom, ya'll!!" We are told that he then showed them his hands and side, presumably so they would actually believe it was the same Jesus, and not a ghost or a demon. And now the reaction is euphoria—"The disciples were overjoyed when they saw the [risen] Lord." At this juncture, Jesus breathes on them and says, "Receive the Holy Spirit" and then adds that whoever's sins they forgive will be forgiven, and whoever's sins they retain will not be forgiven. As we know, Peter was given a similar sort of authority elsewhere (see Matthew 16:19). The crucial point to make about this bequest is that if we have properly read what the Farewell Discourses say, then the disciples did not actually receive the Holy Spirit on this occasion. Jesus had told them before he had to return to the Father in order to send the Spirit to them, and he had not yet done so. He's still on terra firma. We must see this act of Jesus as a prophetic sign act, promising that they will receive the Spirit, and with him empowerment, including empowerment to forgive sins, as Jesus had previously done.

1. What would have been your reaction to the report of Mary Magdalene that she had seen Jesus alive and well?

2. Why do you think Jesus showed his disciples where he had been nailed and pierced?

3. What do you think Jesus meant when he told the disciples that if they didn't forgive someone's sins, they weren't forgiven?

FOUR

Just Another Sunday Night, Until . . .

John 20:24–29 *Now Thomas (also known as Didymus), one of the Twelve, was not with the disciples when Jesus came.* *[25]So the other disciples told him, "We have seen the Lord!" But he said to them, "Unless I see the nail marks in his hands and put my finger where the nails were, and put my hand into his side, I will not believe."* *[26]A week later his disciples were in the house again, and Thomas was with them. Though the doors were locked, Jesus came and stood among them and said, "Peace be with you!"* *[27]Then he said to Thomas, "Put your finger here; see my hands. Reach out your hand and put it into my side. Stop doubting and believe."* *[28]Thomas said to him, "My Lord and my God!"* *[29]Then Jesus told him, "Because you have seen me, you have believed; blessed are those who have not seen and yet have believed."*

Understanding the Word. As it turns out, not all of the eleven disciples had been present at the first appearance of Jesus on Easter Sunday night. Thomas had been elsewhere. And so he missed out on the appearance, and when the male disciples told him about it, he was about as stubborn as the ten had been when Mary Magdalene had reported and not been believed that Jesus had appeared to her.

Thomas says not only must he see Jesus; he must see his wound marks, and not only must he see his wound marks; he must put his fingers into his hands and side! And here is where I say Thomas is *not* depicted as doubting Thomas, but rather he is depicted as unbelieving Thomas. This is exactly what Jesus will say to him: "Stop [disbelieving] and believe!" Thomas is not a person plagued with doubt, or wavering betwixt and between; he simply doesn't believe Jesus has risen from the dead!

When Jesus appears once more, in the same room, in the same fashion, with the same greeting, the only real difference is that Thomas is present. And so Jesus invites Thomas to make good on his statement and touch the healed wounds! The story does not say that in the end he did so, or that he needed to do so. Jesus exhorts him to believe, and finally we get what is ironically the first full confession, the first Christian confession that matches up with the prologue, and proclaims Jesus "my Lord and my God." It may well be of importance that at about the time this gospel was put together, there was an emperor who demanded to be recognized as "*deus et dominus noster,*" "our Lord and our God." If this story is meant to be relevant to that situation, then it would be claiming that the emperor cult is worshiping the wrong person as Lord and God. That would be the risen Jesus!

This story rounds off with Jesus' statement to Thomas: "Because you have seen me, you have believed; blessed are those who have not seen and yet have believed." This last pronouncement is important. It would have been of special relevance to the audience of this gospel in the AD 90s. Most, if not all of them, had never seen Jesus, either during his ministry or as the risen Jesus, and yet they had believed in him. And of course this is also true of all who are writing or reading this. It is certainly one of the major messages of this wonderful gospel that believing leads to seeing, but not only so, those who believe without seeing are more blessed, have a stronger faith. Sometimes we may think, *If I could only have been one of Jesus' original disciples and seen him in the flesh, then I might have stronger faith.* As it turns out, Jesus suggests this is not necessarily true. Faith is the assurance of things hoped for, and you don't hope for what you already have right in front of you.

1. What do you make of the characterization of Thomas in this gospel, who really doesn't figure in the Synoptics?

2. Why do you think we've tended to call him doubting Thomas, when he flatly refused to believe without what he took to be proof?

3. In what sense is Thomas's confession the first real, post-Easter Christian confession?

FIVE

The Purpose of This Good News

John 20:30–31 *Jesus performed many other signs in the presence of his disciples, which are not recorded in this book. ³¹But these are written that you may believe that Jesus is the Messiah, the Son of God, and that by believing you may have life in his name.*

Understanding the Word. These verses probably represent the original conclusion of the Gospel of John. As verse 30 implies, there were many other things Jesus said and did that were not originally included in this gospel. The gospel writer has more material than he needs or can use. One such bit of material that was clearly not a part of the Gospel of John is the much-beloved story of the woman caught in adultery, found in some manuscripts at John 7:53–8:11. The problem is, it is not in our earliest and best witnesses, and it is found in several manuscripts elsewhere in this gospel, and in at least one Greek manuscript it was placed in Luke's gospel! It is a story looking for a home, and I think it is reasonable to assume this is one of those stories that John 20:30 and especially John 21:25 suggests was out there. I have no problem with the idea that it is a genuine story told by the Beloved Disciple; it just wasn't included in the first edition of this gospel, and since original text determines canon, it is not part of Holy Writ. It's probably historically true and certainly true to the character of Jesus, but not an original part of this gospel. Sometimes, one wishes that all of the traditions of the Beloved Disciple had been kept and edited into another gospel, perhaps Gospel of John Part Two, the bonus edition.

In the very last verse of John 20 we have the purpose statement, which can be read in two ways: 1) "in order that you may begin to believe that Jesus . . ." or 2) "so that you will continue believing that Jesus . . ." I would suggest the character of this gospel, with all of its forty-plus parenthetical explanations and other features, favors the former interpretation, though the latter is possible. We are told that the point of such believing is that Jesus is the Messiah, the Son of God—so we might have life in his name. Indeed. We are not called to believe for belief's sake. We are called to believe for salvation's sake. He came that we might have life and have it abundantly. We shouldn't settle for less.

1. Why do you think the gospel writer tells us there are a lot more stories out there about Jesus' signs and teachings?

2. What do you make of the purpose statement?

3. Why would you guess this gospel has been most often translated first of the four Gospels into foreign languages?

COMMENTARY NOTES

Day 2, verse 17. The Greek of John 20:17 is *me mou aptou*, and it does not mean "can't touch this" or "do not touch this." Rather, it means "stop holding on to me." Notice that in Matthew 28:8–10 we are also told that the women, when Jesus appeared to them, grabbed hold of him. He was tangible, and they were thrilled to see him, but there was more for them to do.

Day 3, verse 22. The breathing of Jesus on his disciples fits perfectly with the earlier analogy in John 3 between the Spirit and the wind, or Spirit and breath. The word *pneuma* can mean any of these things. It is interesting to ponder the connection between receiving the Spirit, and the forgiveness of sins. Presumably, what is in view is that one gains the spiritual discernment from the Spirit to know when and how to forgive sins, and whom to forgive and not forgive. Forgiveness is a major theme of the Gospels, and one that distinguishes the new covenant from previous ones. If we reflect on Matthew 18:21–22, we find that this little paragraph has an echo of an Old Testament text. In Genesis 4:24 we hear about Lamech taking vengeance seven times seventy on those who have harmed him. Jesus completely reverses this, in essence calling us to unlimited forgiving. Not just seven times, which Peter must have thought was going on to perfection in forgiveness, but much

more indeed. The point is that we should forgive just as much as God has forgiven us. This is not merely difficult; it's impossible without the presence and power of God in our lives in the person of the Holy Spirit.

Day 3, verse 20 and Day 4, verse 27. Notice as well that Jesus showing his healed wounds on the first Sunday night, and inviting Thomas to touch them on the second Sunday appearance, tells us something important about the risen Jesus. He was in a material body, and he could prove it (cf. Luke 24:39). He was not a mere spirit, they were not just having a mass hallucination, and this was not a vision, collective or individual. The very fact that Jesus appeared to so many different people in different places at different times is important. And this includes his appearing to two people who had not believed in him before his appearing to them: Paul, of course, but also James, his own brother. Notice that in 1 Corinthians 15 we have a list of appearances to both individuals like Peter and to groups of people. None of the Gospels tell us the story of Jesus appearing privately to Peter; it is only mentioned in passing (Luke 24:34). It is inexplicable, if the writers of the Gospels were in the business of inventing stories about whom Jesus appeared to, that they would not have made up a story about Jesus appearing to the leader of the Twelve—Peter. And yet they do not do so.

These stories have all kinds of earmarks of authenticity. Finally, it is worth pointing out that in each appearance scene, *Jesus takes the initiative.* As Paul would say in 1 Corinthians 15, it was not primarily about "we think we saw Jesus alive." It was primarily about "he appeared to Mary, to Simon, to the eleven," and so on. The disciples do not track Jesus down; he tracks them down. The way these stories are framed count against the theory that they are subjective visions.

WEEK ELEVEN

GATHERING DISCUSSION OUTLINE

A. Open session in prayer.

B. View video for this week's readings.

C. What general impressions and thoughts do you have after considering the video, readings, and the daily writings on these Scriptures?

D. Discuss questions based on the daily readings.

   1. **KEY OBSERVATION:** Sometimes when we read these stories, it is too easy to say things like, "Well, I would not have reacted to Mary's testimony the way the eleven disciples did," or "I would not have flatly disbelieved like Thomas did, after all the miracles Jesus performed." We should cut the original disciples, both female and male, a bit of slack. Here we see pictures of them with all their shortcomings and failings, even after the resurrection.

      DISCUSSION QUESTION: How do you think you would have responded to Mary's testimony?

   2. **KEY OBSERVATION:** It is important, said Martin Dibelius, to posit an X large enough to get from the crucifixion to an early church that is bearing witness to a risen Jesus and that is willing to die for its faith.

      DISCUSSION QUESTION: What was it that changed the disciples from fearfully hiding behind locked doors to bold witnesses for Christ?

3. **KEY OBSERVATION:** Sometimes Christians have tended to forget the real gospel, and exchanged it for a watered-down version, for what H. Richard Niebuhr said in *The Kingdom of God in America* (1938): Some people want "a God without wrath, who brought men without sin into a Kingdom without judgment through the ministrations of a Christ without a Cross."

   DISCUSSION QUESTION: How does the gospel presented in the book of John differ from what Niebuhr said some people want?

4. **KEY OBSERVATION:** Sometimes Christians treat their faith as if it is just *Chicken Soup for the Soul*, just nice spiritual messages that give one a sense of well-being. They think history doesn't much matter, but Christianity is a historical religion. Without the historical foundations of our faith, we have no faith. Look, for example, at what we confess in the Apostle's Creed about Jesus.

   DISCUSSION QUESTION: What does the Apostle's Creed say about Jesus? If those things did not happen, what basis do we have for our faith in Jesus?

5. **KEY OBSERVATION:** The New Testament tells us nothing about what Jesus was doing during his down time, the day and a half he was dead.

   DISCUSSION QUESTION: What sorts of explanations have you heard regarding this?

E. What facts and information presented in the commentary portion of the lesson help you understand the weekly Scripture?

F. Close session with prayer.

WEEK TWELVE

John 21:1–25

Jesus' Appearance by the Sea of Galilee

INTRODUCTION

There is really only one continuous narrative in John 21, but it has many dimensions, and we will look at it in some detail. The setting is back at the Sea of Galilee (sometimes also called the Sea of Tiberias, the name given it and the city in the course of Herod Antipas's attempt to curry favor with the emperor). It seems some time has passed since the disciples had been in Jerusalem with the risen Jesus. In addition, only some of the eleven are present, and there are two other disciples, one of whom is the Beloved Disciple. It is an interesting fact that in the Gospel of John, which really does not focus on the ministry around the Sea of Galilee, we have no fishing tales earlier in this gospel, and no call of disciples by the shore of the Sea of Galilee. There is a mention of disciples coming from Bethsaida (Peter, Andrew, Philip, and perhaps Nathanael; see John 1:43–44), but nothing about the calling of the Zebedees to discipleship. Nothing.

If we ask the point of this additional longish narrative in the appendix in John 21, there seem to be several main purposes: to show that the risen Jesus did appear to his disciples in Galilee, even though the earlier focus in John was on events in and around Jerusalem; to recount the restoration of Peter to a place of leadership amongst the disciples; to explain, albeit obliquely, about the Beloved Disciple and his fate; and to explain where the traditions in this gospel came from and that the community vouched for their authenticity. At least the very end of John 21 is surely a much later addition to the materials in John 2–20, because in John 19 the Beloved Disciple is still alive and testifying. The implication from the end of John 21 is that this is no longer the case. The composition history of this book is likely complex, so I will lay out my best hypothesis about it in the commentary notes.

What we learn in John 21 is not only about Jesus' great forgiveness and love; we also learn about Peter's leadership and coming martyrdom and indirectly about the martyrdom of the Beloved Disciple, the respective leaders of the Galilean and Judean groups of Jesus' disciples. Peter was crucified in the late 60s in Rome. We have no idea how the Beloved Disciple died, perhaps of natural causes, as he was very old by the 90s. Nevertheless, he still speaks to us through this gospel, thanks to the extensive efforts and editorial work of John of Patmos.

ONE

Let's Go Fishing

John 21:1–3 *Afterward Jesus appeared again to his disciples, by the Sea of Galilee. It happened this way: ²Simon Peter, Thomas (also known as Didymus), Nathanael from Cana in Galilee, the sons of Zebedee, and two other disciples were together. ³"I'm going out to fish," Simon Peter told them, and they said, "We'll go with you." So they went out and got into the boat, but that night they caught nothing.*

Understanding the Word. There was not much interest in extremely precise chronology in ancient historical and biographical works. People did not walk around with little sundials on their wrists. So when we hear in verse 1 that it was "afterward" when Jesus appeared to some disciples in Galilee, we need not ask how long afterward, as the author had no intention of conveying such precise information. But the word "again" (*palin*) is important, as is the later statement that this was the third time Jesus had appeared to this group of the disciples (twice in Jerusalem on Sunday nights, and then this one). What follows is not a first appearance of the risen Jesus to his disciples, nevertheless verse 12 is odd, as we shall see.

Who's going on this fishing expedition—exactly seven disciples: Peter, Thomas, Nathanael, the two Zebedees, and two unspecified others. It is Peter, as usual, who takes the initiative, and the others say they are coming as well. Fishing was often undertaken at night, and this tale is a good example of that. But indeed, nothing at all was caught. This story should most definitely be compared to the one in Luke 5:1–11, and in preparation for the next segment of the story, it is well if we lay out that text here in preparation for a comparison.

> One day as Jesus was standing by the Lake of Gennesaret, the people were crowding around him and listening to the word of God. [2]He saw at the water's edge two boats, left there by the fishermen, who were washing their nets. [3]He got into one of the boats, the one belonging to Simon, and asked him to put out a little from shore. Then he sat down and taught the people from the boat. [4]When he had finished speaking, he said to Simon, "Put out into deep water, and let down the nets for a catch." [5]Simon answered, "Master, we've worked hard all night and haven't caught anything. But because you say so, I will let down the nets." [6]When they had done so, they caught such a large number of fish that their nets began to break. [7]So they signaled their partners in the other boat to come and help them, and they came and filled both boats so full that they began to sink. [8]When Simon Peter saw this, he fell at Jesus' knees and said, "Go away from me, Lord; I am a sinful man!" [9]For he and all his companions were astonished at the catch of fish they had taken, [10]and so were James and John, the sons of Zebedee, Simon's partners. Then Jesus said to Simon, "Don't be afraid; from now on you will fish for people." [11]So they pulled their boats up on shore, left everything and followed him.

Here is a short list of parallels to consider between Luke 5 and John 21: 1) in both cases it is Peter's boat and Peter fishing, with some help; 2) in both cases they have fished all night and caught nothing; 3) both stories are set at the northern end of the Sea of Galilee; 4) in both cases Jesus tells the disciples to try again, and the result leave him as he was is a huge catch of fish; 5) in both cases the Zebedees are specifically mentioned as Peter's fishing partners. The stories end differently, one with Peter asking Jesus to leave him, as he was a sinful man, the other with Peter being restored by Jesus to leadership among the disciples. How are these two stories related? Is one from the beginning of the ministry relationship between Jesus and Peter, and one from its conclusion? I would simply suggest that either the Beloved Disciple or John deliberately shaped the story in John 21 so that the parallels with the other story would be evident to those who knew the origins of Peter's becoming a fisher of men. Of course, here in John 21, it's not fish but sheep he will be tending and feeding, but in both cases Jesus is talking about Peter evangelizing, teaching, and guiding. The parallels are remarkable, and Peter may be forgiven for having a sense of déjà vu when this transpired with the risen Jesus over breakfast at the sea.

1. Why do you think the appendix was added to this gospel, which ended quite appropriately at the end of John 20?

2. What do you make of the parallels between Luke 5 and John 21?

3. Why would some of the disciples have gone back to Galilee to go fishing rather than waiting in Jerusalem during the days after Jesus ascended and before Pentecost?

TWO

The Light Dawns

John 21:4–9 *Early in the morning, Jesus stood on the shore, but the disciples did not realize that it was Jesus.* *⁵He called out to them, "Friends, haven't you any fish?" "No," they answered.* *⁶He said, "Throw your net on the right side of the boat and you will find some." When they did, they were unable to haul the net in because of the large number of fish.* *⁷Then the disciple whom Jesus loved said to Peter, "It is the Lord!" As soon as Simon Peter heard him say, "It is the Lord," he wrapped his outer garment around him (for he had taken it off) and jumped into the water.* *⁸The other disciples followed in the boat, towing the net full of fish, for they were not far from shore, about a hundred yards.* *⁹When they landed, they saw a fire of burning coals there with fish on it, and some bread.*

Understanding the Word. It is dawn, and Peter and his fishing buddies are still in the boat, still on the water, still haven't caught anything. Perhaps it was the distance from shore, but in any case the disciples do not recognize the man standing on the seashore. He yells to them: "Friends [*paidia*—probably with the sense "young lads" here], haven't you any fish?" When they say no, he says, "Throw your net on the right side of the boat, and you will find some." Without protest, they do as the stranger on the shore suggests, and with dramatic results. The catch is so huge that they can't haul it into the boat. Suddenly, it dawns on the spiritually perceptive one what is going on, and the Beloved Disciple blurts out: "It is the Lord!" No sooner had the Beloved Disciple said this than Peter wrapped his outer garment around him and dove straight into the water, heading for shore. It would appear that Peter had some unfinished business with Jesus, and he desperately wanted an opportunity to be fully reconciled to Jesus and back in his good graces. When a fisherman by trade and inclination says, "To heck with the largest catch ever in the Sea of Galilee" and dives into the water and swims to shore, there is obviously something else urgent on his mind.

Fortunately for the other disciples left with the unenviable task of hauling the mother lode to shore, we learn that they were only about one hundred yards out in the water. And this brings us to a dramatic moment in this story that an alert hearer or reader would not miss. There are only two places in the entire Gospel of John where we hear about a charcoal fire. The last place is here in John 21, but the first place is in John 18:18, where we find Peter warming his hands by a charcoal fire, and about to deny Jesus three times. As I have said before, nothing in this gospel is purely incidental. It has been very carefully put together. Peter denied Jesus by a charcoal fire, and he will be restored beside one. One wonders if Peter himself made the mental connection. In any case, it is not a surprise that what follows is very emotional.

1. Fishing is an enterprise that often requires the patience of Job. Why do you think Jesus initially suggested that he would make the disciples "fishers of human beings"? Which is easier, catching fish or hooking people?

2. In this narrative we see again Peter the impulsive and emotional one, and the Beloved Disciple, the perceptive one, as at the garden tomb. How much do you think pure human personality affects one's relationship with the Lord?

3. Why do you think Jesus called the disciples "lads" or even "little children"?

THREE

Breakfast by the Sea

John 21:10–14 *Jesus said to them, "Bring some of the fish you have just caught."*
[11]So Simon Peter climbed back into the boat and dragged the net ashore. It was
full of large fish, 153, but even with so many the net was not torn. [12]Jesus said
to them, "Come and have breakfast." None of the disciples dared ask him,
"Who are you?" They knew it was the Lord. [13]Jesus came, took the bread and
gave it to them, and did the same with the fish. [14]This was now the third time
Jesus appeared to his disciples after he was raised from the dead.

Understanding the Word. There are some odd features to this story. On the
one hand we have already heard that there was fish and bread on the charcoal
fire Jesus started. On the other hand we hear Jesus tell the lads to bring some
of the fish they have caught, but apparently not for eating. Peter does what
Jesus asks, and at some juncture (probably later) somebody actually counted
the haul of fish. But what is the point of telling us 153 fish were caught, and
large fish at that, as impressive as the number is? This gospel is full of symbolic
tales, and this may be one. There is some evidence that ancient writers thought
there were 153 or so different species of fish in the world. The second-century
Greco-Roman poet Oppian makes a suggestion to this effect, somewhat after
this gospel was written, and the early church father Jerome cites it. Let us
press this for a minute. Suppose the net represents the church, the fish represent fishing for all the different kinds of human beings to bring them into the
net. If this is intended, the Evangelist does not spell it out. It is possible he has
some such subliminal message in mind, not least because it was Peter whom
Jesus first called to be the evangelist of human beings, it was Peter on whom Jesus
said he would found his community, and it was Peter who was the apostle to
the Jews. And we probably see Peter pursuing his calling not only in Acts, but
also in 1 Peter, where we learn that he has been busy in the eastern portions of
what we call Turkey today.

Jesus then feeds the disciples with bread and fish, a typical meal, much
like the one with the five thousand, which likely took place not far from
this locale. The statement that none of the disciples dared ask Jesus who he

was, for actually they knew, seems strange on the surface of things, but it is just possible that to some extent Jesus looked somewhat different than he had before. After all, he now had a resurrection body, not the abused one that the Beloved Disciple last saw him with before Easter Sunday. Clearly there were several things different about him, not least was his ability to appear all of a sudden in rooms, and then disappear. Perhaps this explains this peculiar sentence.

1. Why do you think Jesus asked the disciples to bring him some of the big fish they caught, if, as apparently was the case, they were not going to eat them?

2. Do you think we should see 153 as a symbolic number, or just another example of the stupendous nature of Jesus' miracles in this gospel?

3. Why was a breakfast by the sea an appropriate setting for Jesus to talk to these fishermen?

FOUR

Do You Really Love Me?

John 21:15–19 *When they had finished eating, Jesus said to Simon Peter, "Simon son of John, do you love me more than these?" "Yes, Lord," he said, "you know that I love you." Jesus said, "Feed my lambs." ¹⁶Again Jesus said, "Simon son of John, do you love me?" He answered, "Yes, Lord, you know that I love you." Jesus said, "Take care of my sheep." ¹⁷The third time he said to him, "Simon son of John, do you love me?" Peter was hurt because Jesus asked him the third time, "Do you love me?" He said, "Lord, you know all things; you know that I love you." Jesus said, "Feed my sheep. ¹⁸Very truly I tell you, when you were younger you dressed yourself and went where you wanted; but when you are old you will stretch out your hands, and someone else will dress you and lead you where you do not want to go." ¹⁹Jesus said this to indicate the kind of death by which Peter would glorify God. Then he said to him, "Follow me!"*

Understanding the Word. We've now come to the heart of the matter. There is a progression to what is said here, as we shall see. After they had finished enjoying breakfast together, rather like old times, no doubt, Jesus asks a cryptic question. Notice first that Jesus addresses Peter not by the nickname he gave him (*Cephas* = rock), but by his given name, Simon, and he even adds the patronymic, "son of Jonah/John." Jesus then is starting over with Simon, and he asks, "Do you love me more than these?" This might mean, "Do you love me more than the other disciples love me?" It might mean, "Do you love me more than you love them?" Finally it might mean, "Do you love me more than you love these things?" (i.e., fishing, etc.). In view of the fact that he has just come from fishing, it is very possible that Peter would have understood the question the last way, but it is ambiguous. In any case the point is, Does Peter love Jesus more than all else?

Peter's response is interesting. "Yes, Lord, you know that I love you." Jesus then gives Peter a commission—"Feed my lambs." Again a second time Jesus asks the same question, except we do not have the "more than these" clause attached. Again Jesus calls him Simon son of Jonah/John. And again Peter responds, "Yes, Lord, you know that I love you." The commission this time is a bit different—"Take care of my sheep" (or "shepherd my grown sheep").

Then there is a third question apparently identical to the second (see the commentary notes at the end of this week). "Simon son of Jonah/John, do you love me?" This time Peter is deeply hurt. He begins to weep and responds, "Lord, you know all things; you know that I love you." The third commission then is not merely a call to tend to the mature followers, but to teach them. Jesus has taken Peter through the whole recommissioning process, and it was emotional.

But no sooner had Jesus done this than he tells Peter what is in store for him if he takes up these commissions: "Very truly I tell you," meaning "I'm definitely telling you the truth." "When you were younger you dressed yourself and went where you wanted; but when you are old you will stretch out your hands and someone else will dress you and lead you where you do not want to go." At this juncture we have a comment from John the editor: "Jesus said this to indicate the kind of death by which Peter would glorify God." Like Jesus' death, Peter's death would also glorify God. Peter too would die by crucifixion around AD 68, a considerable period of time before this gospel was written. This section of the narrative tells us that Jesus added, "[Whatever the case, you] follow me!"

1. Why a threefold restoration of Peter?

2. What was Peter being recommissioned to do?

3. What was Jesus implying about Peter's death, and do you think it was reassuring that Jesus suggested it would not happen until Peter was old?

FIVE

Don't Look Back

John 21:20–25 *Peter turned and saw that the disciple whom Jesus loved was following them. (This was the one who had leaned back against Jesus at the supper and had said, "Lord, who is going to betray you?") [21] When Peter saw him, he asked, "Lord, what about him?" [22] Jesus answered, "If I want him to remain alive until I return, what is that to you? You must follow me." [23] Because of this, the rumor spread among the believers that this disciple would not die. But Jesus did not say that he would not die; he only said, "If I want him to remain alive until I return, what is that to you?" [24] This is the disciple who testifies to these things and who wrote them down. We know that his testimony is true. [25] Jesus did many other things as well. If every one of them were written down, I suppose that even the whole world would not have room for the books that would be written.*

Understanding the Word. Peter had been told to keep his eyes on Jesus and follow him. Immediately, Peter turns around, sees the Beloved Disciple, and asks: "Lord, what about him?" Now, it would appear that we have here another little tell-tale sign that all of these stories had independent lives of their own, because the narrator feels he must remind the audience who is the Beloved Disciple (he was the one who reclined with Jesus at the meal where he asked about his betrayal). Now it is telling that this is the reference point, since we know that part of the earliest recorded telling of the Passion Narrative involved the sentence "on the night when Jesus was betrayed" (see 1 Corinthians 11:23). Even young Christians would be expected to be familiar with that story.

Jesus' reply is basically, "That's none of your business; you must follow me." But we have this interesting sentence as well: "If I want him to remain alive until I return again, what is that to you?" which then prompts the quick editorial explanation: "Jesus did not say that he would not die; he only said, 'If I want him to remain alive until I return.'" Notice also that we are dealing with the squelching of a rumor. The rumor had spread that the Beloved Disciple would not die before the return of Christ. Now, I would suggest there was a particular reason why some might be prepared to think this. If, as I have intimated, the Beloved Disciple is Lazarus, Jesus had already raised him from the dead once. You could see the logic being "surely he won't die twice before Jesus returns." But in fact that is exactly what had happened, hence the need for the disclaimer about what Jesus *didn't* say. And notice that this is one of the very rare times Jesus speaks of his return in this whole gospel, which is more vertically than horizontally focused when it comes to the future of Jesus.

Verse 24 is the identity marker—"This [the Beloved Disciple] is the disciple who testifies to all these [wonderful stories], and [fortunately] who wrote them down." And "we know that his testimony is true." This must mean two things: 1) the "we" is the community of the Beloved Disciple, and "his" is the Beloved Disciple; 2) the "we" or a representative of the "we" is doing the writing here. I would suggest we are talking about John of Patmos, from which this gospel takes its name. Notice that the verb "wrote" is in the past tense. The Beloved Disciple is not now writing; he wrote in the past. The community spokesman is writing now, and he put these memoirs together. He adds that "we" all know he testified truthfully. This is a strong reassurance to young Christians who need to know there were eyewitnesses who saw these remarkable events and wrote them down.

The gospel then concludes on a very interesting note; namely, Jesus did so many things, even in a short three-year period of ministry, that there were not enough books then in the world to record all his signs and wonders and teaching. For us two thousand years hence, this remark is a sad one. We would love to know much more about Jesus from the eyewitnesses. There obviously were some extra Johannine traditions circulating in the early church, such as John 7:53–8:11, which didn't make the original editorial cut for this gospel. But we must be thankful for what we have, which is four remarkable, interesting, very different portraits of the one Christ, the one Son of God, the one Savior of the world.

1. Why do you think Peter was concerned about what the Beloved Disciple would do? Why him in particular?

2. Why was the disclaimer needed that Jesus had not said the Beloved Disciple would live until the second coming?

3. Why was the command "you must follow me" so important in the case of Peter instead of wondering about the future and fate of other disciples and leaders?

COMMENTARY NOTES

General Comments. At some point, the Beloved Disciple left Judea for Ephesus after Pentecost, and Jesus' mother went with him. A community was established there that was not a Pauline community, but rather, independent. One of its vital members was a visionary named John, who at some juncture was exiled to Patmos due to his witness for Christ. If he was sent there by Domitian, then he could not have returned to the mainland until his exile lapsed at the end of Domitian's reign in AD 96. Having written Revelation to the Johannine communities in western Asia Minor sometime in the 90s, he returned to Ephesus, discovered that the Beloved Disciple had passed away, and set about to collect the various memoirs of one of the longest living of the original disciples of Jesus. This John of Patmos is the John that Papias calls the older or elder John, and distinguishes him from John son of Zebedee, whom Papias never encountered.

What was needed was a gospel unlike the Synoptics, which by now had begun to circulate throughout the church, especially Mark's (which the Beloved Disciple himself seems to have known, and perhaps John of Patmos did as well). I would suggest that while the Evangelist knows Mark, he does not draw on the account. But he does use it as a frame of reference, and chooses to mainly use different stories when it comes to the miracles of Jesus, avoiding redundancy. He avoids the exorcism tales altogether, and while there

is plenty of wisdom speech and figurative language in this gospel, none of the Synoptic parables show up in this gospel—none. Both of these things are especially strange if this gospel was by a Galilean disciple. The other Gospels were meant to gird up and train those who were already disciples, whether new or old, Jewish or Gentile. John's gospel, however, would be used as a tool for evangelists to draw on in their evangelistic and apologetic work for the faith. John of Patmos thus collected, arranged, edited, and inserted parenthetical clarifications into the Beloved Disciple's testimony, wrote up John 21, and perhaps added the prologue in John 1 as well. The gospel then circulated and soon thereafter had simply the identification "according to John" to distinguish it from the earlier Gospels, which were already extant.

Day 3, verse 11. One of the things one has to be cautious about in reading a highly symbolic narrative like this Fourth Gospel is the danger of allegorizing the text. For example, should we really press the story in John 21 to say that the author was referring to the church by the term "net"—a net that will never break—and that the 153 fish represent fishing for all the different kinds of human beings there were in the ancient world? This borders on allegory, and while there is a lot of figurative, symbolical, and sapiential language in this gospel, we should be cautious about over-reading the text in light of later Christian concerns. It's a matter of following the actual cues in the text, for example, about two levels of discourse, or irony, or double entendres. John's rhetoric is clever and powerful, but he is not an allegorist, and there is not a hidden spiritual meaning under every rock in this gospel. It is, after all, not a fictional work, like Bunyan's *Pilgrim's Progress*. It is rather a historical narrative, with deeper theological significance. There is a big difference.

Day 4, verses 15–17. There has been considerable debate among scholars as to whether or not in this gospel the author uses *agapao* and *phileo* as interchangeable synonyms. Probably most scholars see them as synonyms, based on the fact that earlier in this gospel, both terms are used for God the Father's love for his only begotten Son. While sometimes the two terms seem to be synonyms, that is not always the case, especially when *agapao* or *agape* is used of God's special love, which is certainly more and even different from brotherly love or mere human love. Furthermore, it would be one thing if what we have in the three questions by Jesus using *agapao* and Peter responding in kind, but this is not the case. It is thus possible to read the first two interchanges as follows: "Peter, do you love me with the same divine love that I have loved you?" "Jesus, you know I love you like a brother, the best I can." The second exchange is identical to the first. Peter does not respond in exactly the same terms as Jesus spoke, and frankly, Jesus is not asking about brotherly love here. But the third time Jesus says, "Peter, do you at least love me truly like a brother?" And it

is at that point that Peter breaks down. It is not merely the repetition of the question, it is that Jesus has condescended to Peter's weakness, and asked him about *phileo* the third time, and finally Peter responds in the exact terms Jesus used. I have to believe this difference in terms for love is significant here at least, if not elsewhere in this gospel, simply because of the way the discussion is framed and how the quandary is resolved.

Day 5, verse 24. Scholars have often debated what to make of the "we" here. Who is the "we" and how do they know the Beloved Disciple's testimony is true? The appendix tips us off as to who the "we" is. The allusion to the death of the Beloved Disciple in verses 21 and 22 indicates that the final forming of his memoirs into a gospel was by a hand other than his own. Now, quite rightly, John does not want to claim that this is his own testimony. That is perfectly clear from both what is said in the cross narrative in John 19, and what is said at the end of John 21. These are the Beloved Disciple's memoirs, but formed into a gospel by John. And one must say he did a remarkable, remarkable job. We have said a good deal more about the composition history in the notes above.

Like the Fourth Gospel, this study was done "in order that you might believe that Jesus is the Christ, the Son of God," and if that is already true, that you might wade out deeper into the deep waters of the Johannine presentation of Jesus' story. Can you swim when you are in over your head?

WEEK TWELVE

GATHERING DISCUSSION OUTLINE

A. Open session in prayer.

B. View video for this week's readings.

C. What general impressions and thoughts do you have after considering the video, readings, and the daily writings on these Scriptures?

D. Discuss questions based on the daily readings.

    1. **KEY OBSERVATION:** This gospel is, by intention, deliberately different from the other three canonical Gospels, in part because it does a reading of the story of Jesus in light of earlier Wisdom literature.

    DISCUSSION QUESTION: What other differences do you notice between John's gospel and the other canonical Gospels?

    2. **KEY OBSERVATION:** Throughout this gospel, commandments and love are connected, which is to say obedience and love are connected, for love is commanded. John 21 also suggests that the essential presupposition to doing ministry with and for Jesus is a deep and abiding love of Jesus.

    DISCUSSION QUESTION: How is this demonstrated in John 21, and how does this give you hope?

    3. **KEY OBSERVATION:** The Fourth Gospel puts almost no emphasis on the twelve disciples at all. You have to look high and low to even find a mention of them in this gospel as a collective group chosen by Jesus.

DISCUSSION QUESTION: Who are the prominent people at Jesus' crucifixion in John 19 and at his resurrection in John 20? In addition to the Twelve, what does this remind us about those who were Jesus' disciples?

4. **KEY OBSERVATION:** John 21 is not a mere addendum, a sort of "oh yes, you might find this interesting as well." It is also not the kind of appendix that is like the human one, which can be excised and never missed.

   DISCUSSION QUESTION: What kind of appendix is John 21, and what important information does it provide for us?

5. **KEY OBSERVATION:** Finally, when you get to the end of this gospel, it is time to take stock of what new things you have learned about Jesus, his followers, his critics, and even his executioners. This can lead to reflecting on what you have learned about yourself as a follower of Jesus, and what new things you have learned about your relationship with the Lord.

   DISCUSSION QUESTION: Draw up a chart. What new things can you add that you learned through this study under each of those headings?

E. What facts and information presented in the commentary portion of the lesson help you understand the weekly Scripture?

F. Close session with prayer.